INCARNATE

JESUS AMONG THE BROKEN

INCARNATE

JESUS AMONG THE BROKEN

RICK COLE

[signature]

Capital

Capital

Published by
CAPITAL CHRISTIAN CENTER

capitalonline.cc

ISBN-13: 978-0-9850852-1-6

RELIGION
SPIRITUALITY

Written by Rick Cole

Design and Layout by Jason D. Batt
Cover Design by Trent Ellerman
Cover Photo by Travis Cole

PRINTED IN THE UNITED STATES OF AMERICA

DEDICATION

To my wife, Cathy, whose constant love
and support gives me strength to dream
of ways to express the love of Jesus to others.

To my dad who laid the foundation for me to follow
in wrapping my arms around our city. I miss our times
on the golf course. Your passing has given me a new view of heaven.

To my mom whose prayers and words of encouragement
have given me strength and security for the journey.

TABLE OF CONTENTS

1

THREE WEEKS HOMELESS

I haven't been homeless very long.

Only three weeks, total.

But three weeks is enough.

More than enough.

Enough to change your life.

Enough to change your career, or in my case, your ministry.

Enough to change your worldview.

Enough to change your faith.

Most people who've been homeless aren't like me. I didn't have homelessness thrust on me. I chose it. I'll tell you why.

Also unlike most people who've been homeless, I didn't have to scrape or claw or maneuver my way out of it. All I had to do was go back home. There, I would find a soft bed, and a change of clothes. Fancy suit jackets. A shower. A not-very-new but totally adequate Lexus. A home in Fair Oaks — 85% white, median family income about $88,000, median home value about $479,000, with a homelessness rate of about zero.

If I walked away from homelessness, I had about 4,000 friends eager to hear how it was "out there" — because I was their pastor, and I had just spent weeks living on the streets. Our church, Capital Christian Center, had been founded in 1916 in a lawyer's house and moved into an Oak Park storefront the same year. The next year, they rented a space at 9th and I Streets. In 1922, the congregation gave generously to build a building at 21st and K, then began — like so many city churches of the 20th Century — moving away from the urban center: in 1940 into a new building on W Street, and in 1964 into a newer facility at Howe Avenue and Fair Oaks Blvd. That's where my father, Glen Cole, became the pastor, in 1978.

The ministry grew — and Sacramento kept changing. In 1984, the congregation was happy to move even farther from the center of town, to a beautiful 63-acre campus off of Highway 50, on Micron Avenue. When my father stepped down from the pulpit in 1995, Capital had become the first megachurch in the Sacramento area, and one of the biggest Assemblies of God churches in the nation. I succeeded him as pastor.

Sacramento's urban center kept morphing, enlarging, threatening to engulf us. As in any urban center, there's the matter of crime. Of violence. Of shifting ethnic dynamics. And of course, the matter of homelessness — which, depending on who you ask, is either a cause or an effect of urban decay, if not both. By 2013, Sacramento — California's capital city (which I mention for the benefit of non-Californians) — was "home" to an officially estimated 2,500 homeless people. That figure had more than doubled, to 5,570, by January 2019, a year before COVID, and the pandemic economy.

I guess our church could have kept moving. Fleeing the inner city. Our people have been generous givers. I think if I said "Let's move out," they would have made it happen. But over the years, as I looked at the people of Sacramento — the problems of the city, the needs of the city, the changing economic and ethnic landscape of the city — something in me wanted to stop the slow-motion exodus. It seemed, somehow, that we should stay. We should bloom where we were planted. We should minister to the ones around us. Sort of like Jesus did. Maybe we shouldn't think of Sacramento as "threatening to engulf us." Maybe we should think of Sacramento as beckoning us to be engulfed, and to love.

This was not the conventional megachurch strategy. Don't you want to be in the nicest, most attractive, safest possible neighborhood?

We're not there. Today, Capital Christian Center is a full-on multi-ethnic, multi-national church. From time to time I lead tours to Israel — and I guess it says something about the demographics of our church that on our final pilgrimage tour before the pandemic, 22 of our 31 participants were non-white.

My late father is warmly remembered, and worthy of honor. He was always passionate about "missions." But in his era, "missions" tended to refer to ministry among overseas populations. He was a strong supporter of Mark Buntain's Mission of Mercy in Calcutta and numerous other ministries we called "foreign missions." On the home front, there were the Union Gospel Mission and other ministries to the poor, the homeless, the "underserved" (a term rarely if ever used back then). My father loved helping these ministries, supporting those who were helping people in need. He burned with an impressive passion for empowering people who had a vision to help the needy.

I loved my dad. He planted in me seeds of a heart for the world. And I've found, over the course of my adult life, more and more of a longing to be hands-on in my community as an expression of that heart for the world. Involved personally. In the thick of it — Choose your cliché. Whatever. I'm there. I'm in.

So then came the idea.

2

GET THE PASTOR OFF THE STREETS

Children can teach grownups.

If you ask me to think back to my earliest memories regarding homeless people, they're memories of thinking poorly of "those people." They seemed like people who had made poor decisions. They created their problems, didn't they? *Why don't they look for a job? Why don't they work their way out of these horrible circumstances?* I grew up thinking of myself as a person with compassion for hurting people, but my compassion didn't include the marginalized, the poor, the homeless.

Then I became a parent.

I don't need to tell any parent how a child can change your thinking, but I found that a child can keep changing your thinking, even when that child is no longer a child.

When our oldest son, Nate, grew into his adult years, he influenced my thinking, my focus.

I don't know why, but Nate always seemed to challenge traditional thinking. I do know this: I wanted to stay close to him. So I began to open my mind and heart to other ways of looking at the world. Nate's ways. Instead of judging those who didn't think like me, I started listening. I sought wisdom in how to relate to "the other."

It wasn't just Nate. God kept putting people in my path to challenge my conventional worldview. A sociology professor at the University of Nebraska took an interest in helping me understand the condition of our world for African Americans. (Why a pastor in Sacramento connected with a Nebraska-based professor — and why a Nebraska prof had a life-changing viewpoint on African Americans — is another story entirely.) Thanks to that acquaintance from academia, my perspectives shifted. I began seeing the world less as a place where there are people like me and people who aren't like me — and more as a place where some people have advantages, and others have been marginalized. From this experience, my heart for the African American community grew significantly.

Which led me to a basketball star.

Kevin Johnson was a phenomenal player in the NBA, a darling of all Phoenix Suns fans, in spite of being only an inch over 6 feet tall — short by professional basketball standards. What most of his NBA fans missed was what he did *after* his star-studded three-time All-Star career: He completed his degree in political science at U.C. Berkeley and became Sacramento's first African American mayor. (Along the way, he founded St. HOPE, an after-school program that went on to become an independent charter school district providing high-quality education to nearly 2,000 students.)

One year as Thanksgiving approached and I began thinking about what to preach, I researched what people were doing in our region to serve others. I found news stories about people serving at Loaves & Fishes, our respected local ministry feeding and sheltering the homeless, and stories about other ways people could help feed the hungry. Then I came across an article about our local government attempting to end homelessness.

Mayor Johnson, as he grappled with Sacramento's problems, was assembling a group of community leaders — healthcare and other non-profit providers for the homeless, civic leaders, others. Two seats were designated for clergy. One seat was still vacant. I reached out to the mayor. He was happy to hear from me. I got the last chair.

Sitting in that chair, I was exposed to realities I had never given much thought to. The mayor loved people, and his drive to make Sacramento a better place to live struck a spark in me — not just in me, but in a number of other leaders in the faith community. Mayor Johnson got us thinking about how churches can change communities. How we can invest ourselves and involve ourselves in helping make life better for people.

The mayor asked me, as a member of his committee, to come up with ideas for ways the faith community could respond to the problem of homelessness. I met with my ministry team in our church offices to brainstorm.

The idea God gave us was both simple and complicated: Recruit 30 churches to open their buildings to house 100 to 120 homeless persons from Thanksgiving through the month of March. We figured the homeless could navigate the daytime hours safely; it was the nighttime hours during the winter that could be dangerous. So each evening, the "guests" would meet at a central location downtown and be bussed to whichever church was serving as host for the night. The church family would feed them a hot meal, offer sleeping quarters, provide a continental breakfast in the morning — then the busses would take them back downtown.

This "Winter Sanctuary" worked well. At the host churches, our guests not only enjoyed safe shelter and nutritious meals, but also connections to practical resources — help finding work, for example, and permanent housing. The city and county provided the funds for the infrastructure of the program — primarily buses and security: minimal costs, since the churches donated the food and lodging.

But then came the 2008 recession, and the government funding dried up.

Mayor Johnson wasn't willing to give up on Winter Sanctuary. He asked me if there was any way we could find donations to fund the program's infrastructure. To replace the two-year budget would take $300,000. The only alternative was to let Winter Sanctuary die.

I don't know exactly where the idea came from, but it occurred to me that I might live homeless for a few days, as a fundraising challenge, and to draw attention to the need. *Give to get the pastor off the streets,* this sort of thing. I had pastored the church for nearly 20 years and had never pulled any such "stunt," nothing remotely like it. Such an idea had never even occurred to me before. Come on. What could I be thinking?

I mentioned the idea to my wife, Cathy, no one else. I was actually surprised that she responded positively. She had a sense that it was a God-breathed idea; I wasn't ready to put it in such a lofty category.

A few days later, I met with our team at the church to discuss Winter Sanctuary fundraising possibilities. Brainstorming hadn't been under way long when a staff member offered his idea: *Pastor lives homeless for a few days. Give to get the pastor off the streets.*

Yeah, I said to myself, *maybe Cathy was right. Maybe it's a God thing.*

The more we talked about the idea, the more inspired it seemed. I went to our church's board of directors. These were thoughtful, careful people; I rarely got a unanimously positive response from them on any proposal. This time, there wasn't a hesitant voice in the group. The staff was getting more and more excited. It was rare to find all our leaders in such strong agreement, so on the same page.

The campaign would be called "Rev on the Streets." Our staff set up a webpage and launched a social media campaign to raise awareness and funds. We would aim for $100,000 — a third of the total needed — as a challenge to other churches and groups to contribute the balance.

Logistics?

Back-scheduling from the date when the funds would be needed, we realized that we were already pretty much out of time. I would need to head to the streets in two weeks.

To mount some sort of major orchestration would have defeated the purpose, I guess. Homeless people didn't have much time to map out their move to the streets. They just found themselves there, and they started figuring it out, one day, one night at a time. So that's more or less how I approached it. The staff and I wanted to make it as authentic an experience as possible.

On the other hand, we did do some planning, for safety's sake. A couple staff went with me to scout the downtown area for places I might be able to sleep. We found a somewhat secluded area, about 15 blocks from Cesar Chavez Park, in an alley behind an abandoned industrial building, with a graffiti-splattered wooden fence offering some measure of privacy and protection. A couple slats in the fence were loose, so we removed them and slipped in.

We weren't the first to make this discovery. It was clear that one or more homeless people had already been staying here. We figured it would work for me — if no one got there before me.

I wasn't even homeless yet, but I was already in competition for a place to sleep.

We also scheduled two or three men to stay with me each night — a former police officer, a martial arts specialist, rock singer, others. Both of my grown sons put themselves on the schedule as well. In any case, my companion or companions would generally keep their distance during the day.

I decided I would spend my first night at the Union Gospel Mission, to see what that was like. In preparation, I called ahead to let the Mission leaders know I was coming — and asked them to treat me like they would any other person staying there.

Otherwise, I felt ready to go.

A few nights, maybe a week, that's all I figured on. *Get some media attention, stir up some donations, make the goal, head home.*

I was clueless.

The polite term is *awareness*. I didn't have it. I didn't know I didn't have it, but I didn't have it.

I preached on a Sunday morning, then changed into a hand-me-down sweatshirt and some old clothes in my office, left my wallet and keys, picked up a backpack and a sleeping bag, and walked away from Micron Avenue, across the freeway overpass to the light rail, with my cell phone, my driver's license, and $60 in my pocket. I thought I was prepared to experience homelessness.

I was wrong.

I took the light rail downtown and headed to a coffee shop. I had coffee only; I had decided not to eat the first day, to see how it feels to arrive at Union Gospel Mission hungry at day's end.

By around 3 p.m., I was checking in at the Mission. They gave me a number for a bed, and I sat down in the front yard with 30 or more other men, no one interacting much at all. I felt frustration. You had to stay in the yard or you'd lose your bed number; but the building didn't open till 7 p.m. for the chapel service. Maybe most disturbing of all was that we could see in through the window that someone had the 49ers game on television.

Finally, just before 7, the doors were opened. I had to leave my backpack and sleeping bag in a holding room till the following morning.

I confess that I sat through the chapel service annoyed. It seemed to have an edge of condemnation. We sang some hymns, then heard a message laced with exhortations to make better decisions. At one point, an usher tapped me on the shoulder and told me to remove my hat. A few minutes later, an usher woke a man a few rows in front of me. I guess we weren't allowed to sleep in the chapel service — although I could easily see how it might happen. Some folks sleep to avoid conflict. I felt plenty of conflict. On the other hand, my annoyance — and my hunger — were keeping me alert.

The fact that my stomach was growling put me in a poor position for absorbing any scriptural truths that may have been imparted. I would have loved some bread and fish first — before church. Actually I found myself sitting there thinking *Dang it! Why don't you people read the Bible, and do what Jesus did?* When Jesus wanted to talk to people, He fed them first — 5,000 of them! They were hungry, so He seated them on the ground and multiplied five loaves of bread and two fish. He met their most urgent needs immediately. Only *then* did He make His pitch: If you want to hang around, I've got some things to talk to you about. And everybody stayed! They were drawn to Jesus because He *led with mercy*.

17

We quote this concept of Scripture all the time: Jesus "came and dwelt among us." He lived with us. He understands us. He doesn't lead with the do's and don'ts. He says, "Come to me, all you who are weary and heavy-laden, and I will give you rest." To me, on my first night homeless, *weary* and *heavy-laden* translated to *hungry* — and *rest* translated to *food*.

The service finally ended, and we were ushered into the next room for dinner. I've been asked how the food was. I can't offer an intelligent critique. I was so hungry, it tasted good!

But then came what I can only describe as humiliation: standing in a hallway, one of 50 naked men, in line for the mandatory shower. The guy next to me was a fount of crude sex jokes. I felt horrible, demoralized. Then each us received a bedroll and were sent to our assigned beds, in a big dorm-style room. After the performance of the hyper-sexualized comedian in the shower line, I didn't feel safe overnight.

The next morning, I was eager to leave. I was out the door by 6:30. And I consciously said to myself, *I'm never coming back here.*

Making my way back to Cesar Chavez Park, I started asking other homeless people a simple question — "What do you do during the day?" — which really meant "Where else, besides this park, do you hang out? And where do you go to the bathroom?"

There was one recurring answer: the library! "A lot of homeless people go there," one man shrugged.

Right at the corner, at 9th and I Streets, the library was a welcoming place for the homeless. I was ready for a welcoming place.

It was Monday. It was closed.

Deflated, I walked around some more. Many folks, homeless or otherwise, didn't want to talk. In Cesar Chavez Park, at midday, a church group arrived, handing out food. People rushed to the source. Me too.

In line, I stood next to a 30-something African American woman. I told her I was "new." She was willing to talk. She wasn't the classic homeless person. She was married. But her husband had lost his job. They were struggling to make ends meet. A free lunch was a godsend.

Before long, I had to solve the inevitable problem. Eventually, I found places where I could slip away and relieve myself — whether they were technically legal or not.

That night, my companion from church and I went back to "our" place in the alley. Nobody there — but the previous "tenants" had left a mess. We cleaned out the used condoms, food remnants, and dirty bedding, and barricaded the opening with an empty garbage bin. We created something like an "alarm" bell out of cans and string, attached to a ladder just inside the entrance. I set up an orange and gray dome tent.

The ground is hard, even in a sleeping bag.

The night is noisy. Again and again, throughout the night, people arrived in the alley to scrounge through the contents of a nearby dumpster. Every time someone came down the alley, I started up, my heart racing, my mind on red-alert to any possible danger. When you realize a visitor means you no harm, then you have to try to get back to sleep. More than once, I found myself thinking, *What are you doing dumpster-diving at 2 in the morning? I'm trying to sleep here!*

One night, somebody hoisted himself up to look over the top of the fence and shone a flashlight down at us. "There's people back here!" he yelled. There was the scurrying of footsteps. They moved on. But some version of the scene would be repeated three or four times a night — often accompanied by the urgent question: *Got any pot? Eight bucks!*

Which makes for very, very long nights. I found that I couldn't wait for the sun to come up in the morning. *Please, God let the sun come up earlier today.* I was fine in the daylight. I could see. I didn't feel much vulnerability during the day. Places to go, things to do. But in the night, it feels darker than dark. It feels lonely and it feels heavy and it feels like crazy things go on.

I was never threatened physically. But the fear of it, the unknown, wears you down. Especially in the dark. I never felt fearful during the day; but every single night, there was some sense of foreboding. Several nights, I awakened to fearful feelings. Knowing I had someone with me tended to calm my fears. But most have no protector, no trustworthy companion.

More and more each day, as darkness began descending, I felt a growing uneasiness. *I just want to get through this.*

And for hundreds of people, it happens every single night — while I'm sleeping in my bed in Fair Oaks.

3

GOD BLESS THE LIBRARY

The next morning, I headed straight for the library. I arrived about five minutes before the 10 a.m. opening time. Ten or 15 people were already there, sitting out front with their bags and backpacks and sleeping bags. I sat down next to a fellow, maybe 50 years old, Caucasian, with a small pull-cart. He was completely coherent, and happy to talk. He'd been living on the streets more than a year.

"A couple nights ago, I stayed at the Union Gospel Mission," I told him. "And last night, I stayed in an alley not too far from here. I'm just trying to figure this out. I haven't been here to the library before. Do you do this often?"

"Yeah," he replied. "I actually come here quite a bit."

"What's in here?" I asked. "Like, why's it good?"

The man became a virtual tour guide. He raved about the nice restrooms, and the quiet. He reviewed the contents of each of the library's four floors. He explained the system: If you have an I.D., you can get a library card. (Sweet: I was carrying my driver's license!) With a library card, you can reserve a computer on third floor — free, for an hour.

I was delighted. Civilization! I thanked him.

"Before you go," he said, "let me tell you: A month from now, when it starts getting cold, there's this program over there by Loaves & Fishes, where these buses come pick you up and take you to these churches, and the church will let you sleep there overnight, and give you a really great meal, and people kind of take care of you, and they give you breakfast in the morning. It's a really great thing you should just be aware of, when the time comes."

I wonder what kind of look I was wearing on my face. I almost started crying. He was describing Winter Sanctuary — telling me how much he loved it. The same program I was on the streets trying to save! In that moment, my soul was overwhelmed with joy and gratitude.

"I'll have to check that out," I told him. "Sounds amazing."

Then I went in and got my library card!

I was emboldened. I'd had a good conversation with the woman in the food line. I'd had a good conversation with the man on the library steps. Now, returning to the park, I found a guy, weather-worn, 60-ish, white, sitting on a bench. I sat nearby and proceeded to chat him up.

No response.

I gamely tried again. He gave me a few words.

The more I sat with him, the clearer it was that he was mentally challenged. He could manage a few words, and he was willing to talk, but was struggling cognitively. I realized that he was the kind of person I might have considered scary — because he was "a bit off." But now, just a couple days homeless myself, I found my heart welling up with compassion for him. For the first time ever, I felt a kind of divine sadness. He was facing difficulties — and who knows? Maybe he was one of the "difficult" ones — but *he still mattered.*

4

NOTICING

Of course I couldn't see what was coming. But today, I could draw a line from that moment to this. I could fast-forward from pre-homeless to post-homeless.

By the time I emerged from homelessness, I was ready to be a different person. Ready for change. Ready for freedom from the person I was. The person who thought, *Man, why don't they just get a job? They need to get themselves out of the hole they dug for themselves.* I wanted to be free from the pain of my past: the pain I had borne, self-inflicted pain, the pain of selfishness, the pain of wanting my way ahead of others.

I came away from the streets wanting to live in Philippians 4:4-9 — not just mindlessly quote it: "Rejoice in the Lord always; again I will say, rejoice. Let your reasonableness be known to everyone ... Whatever is true, whatever is honorable, whatever is just, whatever is pure, whatever is lovely, whatever is commendable, if there is any excellence, if there is anything worthy of praise, think about these things."

When I left the streets and headed home, I had lived and worked in the Sacramento area for some 20 years. I had driven through our downtown area countless times. I had driven by the street where Loaves & Fishes serves 800 people a great meal every day. I had walked through Cesar Chavez Park on my way to meetings at City Hall, with a latte in my hand. But in all these criss-crosses of our urban center, I had never seen what was right in front of me.

Then, I became homeless. I started noticing things. I began walking the streets. I walked with the homeless, the mentally ill, the drug-addicted, the alcoholic, the person who's very capable but has suffered a series of problems that left them with no place to sleep or live. I listened.

I also found myself interacting with people who are giving their lives to bring change to people in need, freedom to people in need, help to people in need. But far more often, I found myself ignored. I had ignored multitudes of people over the course of two decades. Now, I was the one ignored. People walked by me like I didn't exist.

I spent my time and energy searching for food and shelter — which means, I had it easy, because I knew my needs would only be short-term; I knew I had friends who would come to my rescue if I got in trouble. The typical homeless person has few such luxuries. I felt fear sometimes; I felt fatigue sometimes; I felt anger sometimes. But I only got the slightest taste of fear and fatigue and anger. It began to dawn on me, on the streets, how someone could become "difficult."

Homelessness seems like an impossible problem. It's easy to become overwhelmed or paralyzed. Not just because of the financial costs, and the overlapping mental and medical and social issues — but because of the perspectives of those of us who aren't homeless. I came away from the streets realizing that I had placed the face of the "difficult" one on *every* homeless person. I was missing the potential to help an enormous population: *everyone else*.

But even the one who's hard to help might be helpable, or might become helpable later. I left the streets beginning to realize that I needed to keep looking for the one who can be helped.

I came away seeing value in even the most troubled soul, recognizing that *there is still a light within them*. They matter to God. Why didn't they matter to me before? They are still a precious child of God. *They must become precious in my sight, too.*

The first chapter of the Gospel of John became real to me. John, in his way, talks about his understanding of who God is, and who Jesus is. I get John better today, I think. Homelessness made me get God better, and get Jesus better.

"The Word became flesh and dwelt among us," John writes, "and we have seen his glory, glory as of the only Son from the Father, full of grace and truth ... For from his fullness we have all received, grace upon grace ..."

The fourth chapter of the book of Hebrews became real to me: "Since then we have a great high priest who has passed through the heavens, Jesus, the Son of God, let us hold fast our confession. For we do not have a high priest who is unable to sympathize with our weaknesses, but one who in every respect has been tempted as we are, yet without sin. Let us then with confidence draw near to the throne of grace, that we may receive mercy and find grace to help in time of need."

I'd been on the streets a few days when I met with a few friends from church. Someone in that conversation used the term "incarnate." *What do you mean?* I asked. "You put yourself in others' shoes," he said.

It was a turning point for me. It's where I began thinking about Jesus — and the homeless — and all kinds of broken people — in a whole new way. I began seeing John 1 and Hebrews 4 differently, because I started seeing what God did for me in a different way. *Incarnation* isn't just a fancy theological term for me anymore. Jesus *incarnated*. He came into my world. He pulled on my shoes. He experienced life like I do. All of it: the hurts, the pains, the sorrows. If anybody understands what you're going through, Jesus does.

Jesus knows where we're weak — but He doesn't condemn us for that. His grace covers us. He hasn't come to push us away. He came to bring us in. He came to shelter us. He came to love us. Not to put us under pressure; not to cause us trouble. He came to resolve our troubles. He came to take the pain, all that we would ever have, on Himself. He came to take our place. He says, "I want you to be healthy. I want you to be well."

But He doesn't just say this to Rick Cole. He doesn't just say this to white people or employed people or "normal" people. He says it to every person wandering the streets homeless. Every person hunched on a bench in Cesar Chavez Park. Every person I used to drive past on my way to visit Loaves & Fishes, without seeing them. For 20 years, they were invisible to me. I couldn't remember a single soul from those two decades. They were not on my radar. I had something else to do. They were not my concern. Basically, they were not people to me. I had my latte, and my ministry appointments.

Or if I noticed them at all, it was: They can't be helped. They're mentally ill. They want to be out there. They don't want a place to stay.

Or: What can you do? It's drug addicts and alcoholics and prostitutes and criminals. They made their bed, let them lie in it. It's their problem.

Or: All those people, living off my taxes. Why don't they get a job? What's wrong with them?

Until now, for a few extraordinary days, I saw them. I was with them. They became human beings. It wasn't about the concept of homelessness. It was about people. The people Jesus came for. The people His *incarnation* was for.

Why do I put people down, when the true incarnate One experienced all of this depravity and didn't put anyone down? The transformation God wants for me is not just for me to be saved — it's also a transformation in how I interact with people. In the Church, down through the centuries, we've missed this. The more religious we get, the more judgmental we get, the more off-putting we are to people who aren't like us. We've missed the mark of Christ's heart.

If we could grasp the incarnation — Jesus showing up, taking our place, sharing in our troubles, advocating for us — it would transform how we view ourselves, and Him, and *others*. He understands us. He understands our weaknesses, so He's not put off by us. He understands our failings. He understands our brokenness. He has felt our pain. He even experienced what our temptations are like. On the cross, He actually bore all our sins, all our sorrows. He actually felt it in that moment — the burdens of every person who's ever lived. It all got placed on Him.

Jesus never said, *Man, get your act together.* That's what I say, but it's not what He says. He says, *I got it together for you, and I'll help you, if you just let me into your world. I want to make things better for you.*

My negative view of broken people — not just the homeless, but the addict, the hate-filled person, the repeat screw-up, the "problem person," everybody who isn't as "right" as I think I am — that negative view has to change, when I realize that Jesus did His *incarnation* thing for me *and* for them. In fact, it's not *them* and *me*. It's us.

Can I think about the good and the praise-worthy and the pure and the lovely, as Scripture calls me to, even when I'm thinking about a homeless person? When I'm complaining about the inconvenience or the cost of homelessness? A change begins in me when I realize that I'm the one rescued by the incarnation of Christ, I'm the one whose pain He came to take, I'm free because of Him — not because I've figured it out, but because *He* figured it out. I'm just the recipient of His love, His grace, His mercy. It's the amazing gift of life.

I want to be free from my prison of negativity. I want to escape the rat race and embrace the spiritual gift of slowness. We live in a fast-paced, noisy world. Every day is filled with work deadlines, dropping kids off at soccer practice, trying to keep up with the proverbial Joneses. But the speed of life can keep me from hearing the voice of God. Distraction and escapism keep me from dealing with my spiritual brokenness. Busyness is a badge of honor in our culture — when it *should* be a sign that I might be avoiding something important. Perhaps the way to freedom is to stop saying "I'm busy" and start telling God, "I'm ready."

Can I look at my blind spots? Can I inspect the areas of my life I've been neglecting? Can I finally examine my life and be honest with myself? Maybe everything isn't so perfect? Maybe I don't have it all figured out? Maybe we do hurt? Maybe we do need God's freedom? Maybe there's a siren going off that I need to pay attention to? Maybe these questions are the first steps to finding freedom?

Maybe it's time to say, "God, I'm ready."

5

A DOG IS BETTER

B y my fourth day of homelessness, I was starting to look the part. Reporter Cynthia Hubert interviewed me for the *Sacramento Bee* newspaper, and confirmed it.

"Beneath a black baseball cap, his face was pale and unshaven," she wrote. "His eyes were bloodshot and weary, framed by deep creases ... wearing jeans and a blue hoodie, and contemplating where he might clean up and brush his teeth. He had last showered on Sunday, in a communal facility at the Union Gospel Mission. He had not eaten since Tuesday, when he had chicken noodle soup and a sandwich with hundreds of others at the Loaves & Fishes homeless services complex on North C Street. It was farmers market day at Cesar Chavez, and the aroma of kettle corn and jumbo hot dogs were starting to make Cole hungry."

I told her honestly what I had learned so far: "Homelessness strips you down. It's dehumanizing. I think this experience will help me grow in my compassion for people and see the world in a different way."

It was already happening.

It felt like Cesar Chavez was becoming *my* park. The homeless people lining the perimeter weren't just placeholders anymore. They were becoming my people. I didn't foresee this. But it's what God had in store for me.

I learned as I went. It wasn't what I expected. I thought I would have to deal with hunger, for example, but I found that most of the homeless weren't often hungry. There was food available; they knew where to go. You could go to Loaves & Fishes, for instance, and get a good meal. And various groups occasionally showed up in the park and offered free food. The unemployed homeless also typically get a little government assistance cash; it doesn't go far, but they can grab a sandwich from time to time.

My "planning" wasn't very effective; I hadn't thought ahead enough about what I would bring with me. When I looked later — after my first-day Starbucks — at the initial $60 I had in my pocket, I was mildly horrified. In five frivolous minutes, I was already down to $55.

Over the next few days, I got hungry a couple times. If I didn't have other options at the moment, I reluctantly pulled out my meager supply of cash and bought cheap fast food. I had become part of that world — not destitute, necessarily, but a world of diminishing choices, and rarely a world of good health. I had the faculties, mentally and financially, to navigate this world. Many others didn't.

Where will I sleep? How long before the cops run me off?

What will I eat? How can I afford it?

Where can I go to the bathroom, where I don't have to be a customer? Can I hold it from 5 p.m., when the library closes, till 10 a.m., when the library opens? What about Monday (dreaded Monday) when the library is closed?

Who will accept me? Who will reject me?

A man on the street advised me that homelessness is especially challenging — even dangerous — for women. Most homeless women, he said, will either find a man to partner with on the street, or a dog.

"Most figure out," he added, "a dog is better."

6

KEEP ME SLOW

We Christians are fond of saying "Don't judge."
We're fond of saying a lot of things.
We do words.

But I came away from homelessness ready for change. Change comes through action, not words.

I've found that the more we talk, the more we tend to condemn. It's natural. If we pause — if we stop talking, and start listening — if we scale back on the talk, and scale up the action, motivated by love — our actions will accomplish more than our words ever could.

What can we *do* to lift up the hurting and the broken-hearted, and make a difference in their lives?

God didn't settle for words. When He wanted to bring change to the world, He jumped right in the middle of it. This is what John 3:16-17 is really about: "For God so loved the world, that he gave his only Son, that whoever believes in him should not perish but have eternal life. For God did not send his Son into the world to condemn the world, but in order that the world might be saved through him."

Change comes through action, not words. God uses action to bring change — and show the way to freedom.

Some are living lives of action. I found a few. Like the day I was wandering, experiencing the dilemma of pointlessness. What do you do when you don't have a job? I didn't have a job, for the first time in my adult life. I had no appointments. I didn't look at my calendar once.

What am I going to do today? I don't know.

I think I'm going to go see if I can get a free lunch at Loaves & Fishes.

Out on the street there, I bumped into Sister Libby. She's a longtime friend of mine; she served on the mayor's committee with me. She's run Loaves & Fishes for many years.

"Is this your first time here?" she cried. "We love our guests! Right down here, you get your meal ticket. Are these folks with you? I can explain everything you need to do."

I was thinking, *Do I look that bad already?*

I found a way to speak to her privately. "You know what I'm doing here, right?"

She smiled a bit sheepishly. "Yes." Then she went back to doing her job.

In that moment, I realized: Yes, she did know me, but she didn't want to give any preference to one guest over the others. I loved that.

I got in line and got my number. I was somewhere in the 500s — they feed 800 every day.

Mustard Seed School is there too, part of the inner-city Loaves & Fishes operation — a school for homeless children. I fell into conversation with one of the school's leaders and learned that she had been homeless herself. It was through that experience that she felt compelled to start helping children. Today she's teaching and training teachers.

"I hoped I would see you here!" she said.

I was puzzled.

"See you on Sunday!" she added.

My face must have told her how confused I was.

"You know I go to your church, right?" she asked with a big smile.

I did my best to recover. "Uh, yeah!" I replied. "That's awesome! I'll see you Sunday!"

It warmed my heart to learn that a member of our church was leading at the Mustard Seed School for homeless children — *she's out there taking action.*

I've come to believe that God has something for everybody — a way to help people in need. It's not the same thing for everybody. This isn't a guilt trip; it's just God's design for life. *We incarnate — like Jesus did.* We step into the life of someone in need, help to ease their burden. Those who are blessed share the blessing with those who need a blessing. Along the way, Jesus says, "We can do this together." His love changes lives.

I thought I was on the streets to draw awareness to the homeless, and raise some money. The experience of walking among "the least of these" turned my world upside down. I started feeling what "the least of these" feel. Not as deeply as they do; not for as long as they do. But it was a beginning.

Keep me slow. That's how I began to pray. I used to drive fast everywhere. Now, on foot, I had finally slowed down enough to notice people. Walking miles a day, visiting people and groups helping the homeless, to see what they do and how, I found beauty in people. Soon, I knew, I would return to my regular life. I began praying I wouldn't speed up again and bypass people in need. In fact, I needed to become one of the people helping them.

7

MIRACLE MATTRESS

I didn't sleep every night on the ground. God gave me a miracle mattress.

One day my companion was Jacoby Shaddix, the tattoo-covered lead singer with the group Papa Roach who had recently come to faith in Jesus. ("Maybe I should get a tattoo to commemorate this whole experience," I joked. "Sweet!" he replied. "I'll show you where to go!") Jacoby and I arrived at my little hiding place, just off the alleyway between the abandoned building and the wretched wooden fence, when suddenly we heard a truck pulling up.

Jacoby jumped up to peer through the slats of the fence. The guys in the truck were wrangling an old mattress.

"What are you doing?" Jacoby called.

"Dumping this mattress."

Jacoby didn't hesitate. "Can we have it?"

"Sure."

"Sweet!"

He pulled the mattress through the fence and into our space. We bent the mattress in two, shoved it through the door of our tent, and let it go. *Boing!* It sprang flat onto the tent floor. It fit perfectly. *Manna from heaven!*

Jacoby started shouting: "Thank you, God! Whenever I'm with the Rev, miracles happen!"

It was luxurious. I slept on a mattress the rest of my time in that alley. Was I "cheating"? I told myself no — because it was a miracle from heaven! Hey, when you walk with God, even when you're in the midst of troubles, good things happen. That's the story I told myself, and I'm sticking with it. I'm riding the blessing of His grace!

8

GRUMPY GOD

Everyone's a critic. You've heard this saying. The reason you've heard it is that it's basically true.

We human beings tend toward a critical nature.

Criticism — judgmentalism — they're intertwined. I judge you, I criticize you. I'm making myself right in my own mind. I'm making you wrong. Making you somehow unworthy.

Criticism has become epidemic in our culture. Especially with the advent of social media, just about everyone's a critic — literally. We spend phenomenal amounts of time and energy *dividing:* separating the critic from the unwanted.

I'm ready for freedom from all that. I want to be free from seeing the worst in everything instead of the best. I want to be free from negativity. I want to be free from selfishness and self-praise.

I want to rejoice in the Lord always.

I want to think on these things — the true, the noble, the right, the pure, the lovely, the admirable, the excellent, the praiseworthy. I want to experience what Paul promised at the end of that famous scriptural passage: "And the God of peace will be with you."

Well, wrong is wrong. Some things need to be judged. Some things need to be criticized.
We need to get off our high, stinky, religious horses.

We need to stop griping and complaining and pointing fingers at everybody who's "screwing up the whole world."

We need to point that finger back at ourselves and say, "I'm a screw-up. I need help. I need grace. I need Jesus. Nobody is worse than me."

If I can start to see the world this way, I'll begin to be transformed myself — and peace will start to come into my life.

If I start going out of my way to touch the person who's in my way — instead of trying to get around them, instead of ignoring them, instead of treating them as a non-person — if I begin to see the value in every person, even the "crazy" one, even the person who can't carry on a conversation with you — I'll be transformed. And the world will be changed.

I had a little taste of transformation when I was homeless. Pretty soon there wasn't a person in that park that I didn't see value in. I saw a little light in every soul. I saw that there's something God-placed in every person — because He created every one of us. Yes, something went wrong in their lives along the way, and it's sad. But instead of blaming it on them — or blaming the government — or blaming the "system" that's perpetuating these problems — if I get up and go, and befriend that person, if I look at them in the eye and love them, if I can find a pathway to help the ones who *can* be helped, and love the ones who can't — what happens? I'm transformed. And the world is somehow changed.

Feeling guilty? Since that day, I've had to repeatedly monitor my own criticism impulse. Someone who's never lived out on the streets, even for a few nights as I did, can't be expected to respond the way I think they should. I've worked hard not to react to other people's point of view about my experience, because they didn't experience what I experienced. I grew up in my dad's church, where we often welcomed missionaries serving in other countries, other cultures. I heard their stories. It was possible for a missionary to slather guilt on people. The missionary was out there in a raw situation; the congregation is living in a place of comfort. It's hard for one party to understand what the other party considers obvious. So I understand the disconnect. To this day, some folks don't respond to the issue of homelessness, the problem of broken people, the way I do. My heart hurts, but I don't respond with rage. I can't. If I did, I would be missing my own point. I was there myself.

But I left the streets with the faces of the homeless on my mind. I couldn't escape them. It was a strange new world for me. I didn't want it to change. The idea that every soul matters was revolutionary for me. Inspiring. Energizing. Thrilling. I came away buzzing with a passion to offer hope — although at the moment I didn't have a clue how. All I was sure of was that I was ready for change.

No more "grumpy God." I want to live in the joy of John 3:17 — "For God did not send his Son into the world to condemn the world, but in order that the world might be saved through him." God looked down from heaven and saw the big train wreck of humanity — *Hey! Everybody on the train is someone I love!* But His response wasn't just to say something, offer some consoling words, some hopeful words, some profoundly wise words. No. He acted. He gave His best.

And His best was Jesus. And Jesus did likewise. He acted. He died on the cross, took everybody's shame, everybody's loss, and offered a better life. All we had to do was let Him.

Our culture has gone more in the direction of criticism, away from the direction of grace, than at any point in our lifetime. We have leaders proclaiming, *If you're not like me, you're wrong.* I don't think this is the Jesus approach. We are called to be encouragers to help people be their best. Criticism is today's baseline, our default response. But it's not God's way.

We need a spiritual viewpoint, not a secular viewpoint.

Criticism rarely helps. If I criticize the poor, if I look down on them, if I denigrate "the least of these," I am making fun of God.

This is not a question of approving someone's ideas, someone's lifestyle, someone's worldview. This is, at its heart, what a child learns in preschool: *kindness.* Which looks more like Jesus.

9

WHAT YOU NEED

Four of the most dangerous words in the English language: *What you need is …*

We say these words, or think them, at least subconsciously, many thousands of times over the course of our lives.

We see someone in need, and we assume we understand their need. Then we assume we know the solution to their need.

If the homeless would just get a job …

And because they're not doing what we imagine they ought to be doing, we think less of them. We consider them inferior.

On the streets, I found that I wasn't just wrong in various ways about broken people, I was wrong in *layers*. For example: My assumption about people "just wanting to live out there" was wrong — many didn't want to be living out there. But beyond this error, I found that some *did* want to live "out there"; and — here came the big revelation for me — *those people still had value, too.* Yes, some folks have come to feel better living out on the streets than living what most of us would consider to be a conventional life. But this doesn't mean they deserve our contempt. In fact, it doesn't mean they deserve to be written off as

41

unhelpable, or unworthy of help. *They are still worth reaching out to.* There may be a way to help them, to express God's love, to make a positive difference in their lives.

What can I do to show this person they matter? Is this person one of God's children? Yes. Then can I be kind to them? Isn't there something in my spirit that can reflect the love of Jesus to them?

Our tendency is to stand back. To talk about the need for change. But not to do anything to create change. We discuss the subject, rather than engage the subject. We point fingers at the politicians, never at ourselves. We lay blame elsewhere.

Here's something else we say, or think: *Figure it out.* You're addicted? Figure it out. You're jobless? Figure it out. You're homeless? Figure it out. What we never-yet-addicted, never-yet-jobless, never-yet-homeless people don't realize is that some problems, once you have them, aren't easily figure-out-able. Yes, maybe he was a fool to get addicted — I've been a fool in a lot of ways too, over my lifetime. Getting addicted just wasn't one of them, thank God. But once you're addicted, it becomes a disease that you can't simply "get out of" by yourself. Yes, maybe she was a fool and that's how she lost her job. Yes, maybe they were foolish and that's how they became homeless. But many today, in the world after COVID, are jobless *without* having been foolish, or homeless *without* having been foolish.

And on top of all this, maybe most important of all, *God doesn't sort us on the basis of how we got into our mess.* We human beings do this kind of sorting, not God. He just loves people in messes — and wants to help.

My contempt for broken people may not be conscious. Especially after a lifetime of it, I can keep it buried deep in my brain. This is how people in need become invisible to me. I remember first hearing about Loaves & Fishes, years ago. Some time later, I was in my car, in the downtown area, and I decided just to drive by and see where it was on the road. *Oh yeah, there it is.* I didn't get out of my car. And I never got out of my car. Until I was homeless, nearly 20 years later, I had never once stepped out of my car and walked down that street to see what was happening, or who the people were. They were invisible to me.

But to be kind to a broken person, to be proactive in seeking to help, doesn't mean jumping in and imposing a fix on them. *What you need is [fill in the blank]* isn't the answer. I have to be careful, thoughtful. I have to listen first. Develop a relationship. Discern not only the need, but that person's readiness and openness.

It can be hard. Maybe even impossible. There are folks who are truly out of their mind. Something happened in life, maybe even before their birth, that took away their ability to function. But God still loves them; I want to, too. Maybe there are limits to what I could do practically. But if my heart is at least soft, I'm in a better place. And if my heart is soft, then *if* there's something I could or should do, I'll be better able to hear it, see it, sense it. If my heart isn't soft, I'll be deaf to anything God might prompt me to do to help a hurting person. Along the way, I am sure of this: To berate a broken person, to put them down, isn't God's way.

To be honest, I find that I need to apply the same kind of restraint in dealing with people in my own world, the world of bounty, when they express antipathy or even apathy toward the homeless and the broken. *What you need is* isn't the answer here either.

My fear in writing this book is that it will be misunderstood as a scolding. That's not my intent. I do believe that God's heart breaks for the broken, and we will align ourselves more with God's heart if our hearts break for the broken as well. I believe it will be healthier for us spiritually, and the world will be a better place — but what form this godly response takes I can't dictate. So when I hear someone define the homeless in contemptuous terms, I can't judge. I can't lash out. All I can do is grieve. I do hear it — it sounds loud and harsh, in my spirit — I have an anxiety response to it. There's a friction between my heart and that person's heart. But God still loves the person who hates, or the person whose heart is hard, or the person whose heart is cold, or the person whose heart is simply unaware.

I recommend contact. Physical, human, face-to-face contact. Volunteer at a shelter. Serve in a food line. Take a day to sit in the park and strike up conversations. When you put a face on an issue, it moves from *issue* to *people*. It becomes harder to generalize, because you're now talking about a person, not an "issue" or a "problem" or a "disease" or even "those kinds of people." You don't think in the same terms. It's no longer *homelessness*. It's Henry. It's Loretta.

10

STAYING

It is what it is — until it isn't anymore.

What began as a fundraising campaign didn't stay just a fundraising campaign.

God was at work, on multiple levels.

In me, His work was going strong. But in the fundraising realm, He was also at work. Our church team's social media outreach inspired many to give generously. Media coverage in the Sacramento market and beyond inspired many additional donations.

Within a few days, we were roaring toward our $100,000 goal, and beyond. The money we wanted to contribute toward the $300,000 need, to keep Winter Sanctuary going — that money was raised in a week.

Which should have meant I could go home.

I wanted to go home. I wanted it badly. My wife, my house, my bed, my fridge, my shower, my closet of clothes, my normal life.

But by the time I could, I couldn't.

I was deeply conscious of feeling more and more weary every morning, waking less and less refreshed. Homelessness was taking its toll.

But I couldn't go home.

We might have fulfilled our fundraising objective, but God seemed to have another objective.

I was experiencing something that I hadn't expected.

Something had started in me, something that needed finishing.

Something was changing in my heart.

What started as a "task" was no more. This was about life now. I was beginning to see the world through different eyes. I was feeling people's sorrows.

I could go home, but I can't go home.

I looked around at my new world, the once-invisible people who were now so visible and real and close to me, and it didn't feel right to make an exit. I peered into my own heart, and saw something happening there, deep in my spirit, and it didn't seem finished.

It's not just about the money. That's part of it, but not the most important part. It's bigger than keeping Winter Sanctuary going. It's about getting me going — in a new direction. Along a new trajectory. With new eyes. New energy. New purpose.

Not that it was pleasant. It wasn't. I was beginning to feel pain I never knew before, never knew existed. I was beginning to sense people's loneliness, beginning to feel the sorrow of their journey — where they couldn't find any end in sight. I wasn't ready to peel off, back onto my own comfortable road.

I can do a few more days, I told myself. It wasn't a heroic thought. I wasn't some sort of martyr. My few days of homelessness was really not a big deal compared to what hundreds and hundreds of people were going through on the streets of Sacramento. But I just felt somehow that I needed a few more days.

I talked with Cathy. She immediately agreed. She sensed a spiritual directive. Not that she liked it. *I hate it, but I get it.*

I would stay on the streets.

I was still stuffing a lot of my own emotions. I was still having so many first-time experiences. I was still trying to figure everything out. I was still watching this new life unfold every day, still sensing God at work in me. I was still, in a lot of ways, so confused. Still carrying a burden, and not really understanding it.

I guess all my life, I'd been misunderstanding the whole idea of *misunderstanding.*

11

MISUNDERSTOOD

You've been misunderstood, of course. Me too. *How can you see me that way? All of us have been through it. How could you make such a choice? How can you hold such a view?*

Jesus knows all about it. He was misunderstood.

When He walked this earth, people were endlessly trying to figure out who He was.

Some worshiped Him and followed Him till He was seen as a threat. He was put to death — sure, totally in God's plan and purpose, but also the result of great misunderstandings about who He was.

In Luke 23, Jesus meets two politicians, Pilate and Herod. It goes badly — because of misunderstanding.

The religious leaders haul Jesus before Pilate. They're hot. They're making accusations. So Pilate asks Him, "Are you the king of the Jews?"

Jesus gives him a curious answer: "You have said so."

Pilate shrugs. "I find no guilt in this man."

The religious leaders won't let it go. Pretty soon it comes out that Jesus is a Galilean. The light bulb goes on over Pilate's head. This case belongs in

Herod's jurisdiction! He can send him over to Herod. What a fortuitous coincidence: Herod happens to be in town.

Herod's happy. He's heard about this guy. The miracle-worker! Let's see some magic.

But when Herod tries to engage Him, Jesus offers "no answer."

The religious leaders go berserk. They ramp up the pressure. Herod isn't Pilate. Herod is impressionable. He gets heated up himself. His soldiers camp on. Everybody's snarling at Jesus, mocking Him. Herod puts a fancy outfit on Him, to make Him a laughingstock, and sends Him back to Pilate. It's a political move. Herod and Pilate have been at odds — but now Herod is giving Pilate the photo opp. (It works. The two politicians bury the hatchet after this and become buddies.)

The only wrinkle is that Pilate doesn't have enough evidence against Jesus to do what the religious leaders want, which is to execute Him. He can punish Him, sure, but then he'll have to release Him.

The gang screams. They want a prisoner exchange. The murderer and insurrectionist Barabbas is in jail; they'll take him instead, as part of the traditional Passover prisoner-release. Pilate can't calm them down. He finally caves. Barabbas is out; Jesus is slated for flogging, then execution.

What was making the religious leaders so crazy? They misunderstood, in more ways than one. They thought the Messiah would appear and set up an earthly kingdom. They also thought Jesus was angling to seize earthly power, to set Himself up as the human ruler over the Jews — but not as part of the established Jewish hierarchy, which would wreck the religious leaders' cushy status.

What was Pilate's perspective? When he asks "Are you the king of the Jews?" he's asking, "Are you a politician? Are you looking to rule? You think you're the guy with all the power?" Jesus' ambiguous answer is basically, *You say so.* It's not a yes. It's not a no. It's brilliant.

If Jesus says *yes*, Pilate will have a problem with Him. Jesus becomes a usurper of political power.

If Jesus says *no*, He dumps off His role as the ruler of the universe for all eternity.

So He doesn't say *yes* or *no*. He only says what's true.

Jesus could have lifted a finger and exerted His power and shown what He possessed, and they would have all been dead. He had the power to strike them all. *Boom*, in an instant. He had the power to do that. They didn't know that. They wouldn't have asked Him that if they believed He had such power. Yet here is the most powerful person in the room saying, *I'm going to wait this out. I'm not going to demand. I'm not going to coerce. I'm not going to control. I'm going to give myself.* And He showed what power looked like in that choice.

One little wave of His hand could have just toppled everybody in the room. Pilate could have gone to his eternal demise had Jesus wanted that. He had that power, but He had the power to do something bigger than to harm. Bigger than to control. Than to seize the moment. It wasn't the moment Jesus came for to establish an earthly kingdom. No, He came to establish an eternal kingdom. One that's better and bigger and outlasts anything that happens on this earth. We're pilgrims passing through. This is very temporary. And how we serve Jesus is what matters in this moment that we're in.

Jesus was hugely misunderstood. Pilate and his entourage, Herod and his entourage, the religious leaders — nobody understood Him.

We need to.

We need to understand that politicians are not our saviors. We need to learn to walk in the power of God's love. We need to learn to live out our faith in the world in which we find ourselves. Because lives are at stake. Someone's future is in the crosshairs. Eternity hangs in the balance. *What kind of influence does God want His people to exert in the world?*

The human political system is often used for self-promotion and coercion: *I am the strongest, and I will control you.* Jesus revealed a different kind of power. He gave up His reputation. He humbled Himself. He operated on *servant* wavelength. He refused to defend Himself. He didn't hold on to what He deserved. He made sacrifices. He had an endless list of rights, but He gave up His rights out of a desire to let love win.

Jesus shows us that real power is changing people, not controlling them.

We see in our own world today how poorly the human "control" system works. People don't take kindly to being controlled.

Jesus is still misunderstood. In John 12, He says, "And I, when I am lifted up from the earth, will draw all people to myself." Many think He's talking about being lifted up in worship. No. He's talking about being lifted up on the cross: sacrificed. He's talking about drawing people not by His power to control, but by giving Himself up, taking on the sins of the whole human race. Your failures and mine. Every failure represented by every person languishing in Cesar Chavez Park.

He had plenty of power, but He wasn't satisfied with the idea of forcing us into anything. He wanted to change us from the inside, to change our hearts, to change our view of the world, to change our view of other people — *so that we too would desire to serve them, not control them.*

So that we would become Jesus to our world.

To accomplish such a goal, He couldn't force us. He could only offer Himself to us. I can choose to let Him change me. I can give myself to Him and let Him guide me by His love, His wisdom.

I want to change somebody? I want to see them change? Then I'll need to get vulnerable, too. If I want to see people change, I have to sacrifice. I have to spend time with them. I have to get to know them. I have to sacrifice of myself in order to earn their trust, so they can see there's something new that can happen inside. So they can encounter what it looks like to follow Jesus through our example.

It can't be *I have the answers, so follow me.* Control and self-promotion go together. *When you see my greatness, you want to do whatever I tell you to do.*

Change and self-sacrifice go together. *If I give myself up, make myself vulnerable, show someone what love really looks like, maybe they'll embrace His love — and they'll change.*

12

SOLVE IT WITH MONEY

My place off the alley, behind the wooden fence, wasn't mine forever. A couple nights in, when my companion and I arrived, it was clear we'd had a visitor. The garbage can barrier and tin-can alarm system were gone. My orange and gray dome tent was balled up outside the enclosure.

My companion for the night was Tom Platina, a local police officer who served in Security at our church. He slipped through the wooden slats and found the new tenant: a woman, curled up on a "bed" of wooden pallets and covered with blankets.

"Come out!" he shouted. "We don't want to hurt you! Do you have any weapons? I'm serious. I have children!"

A slight, barefoot woman emerged, wrapped in a blanket. She was disheveled and sad-looking.

I didn't want to kick her out. But we also couldn't share the space with her. *Who knows who might be joining her later tonight?*

Tom and I came up with a plan — definitely the kind of scheme that "civilized people" jump to: a plan involving money.

We offered to book her into a nearby motel.

She agreed sullenly.

"Meet me there," Tom instructed her. We would restore order to our hovel, then he would pay for her room.

The woman stumbled down the alley and into the street. A few minutes later, Tom was on his way. But before long, he was back.

She had never shown up. She was gone, who knows where.

In the endless chess match of Where To Sleep, I had won a game. But it didn't feel good.

13

No Bath

My wife was patient. More than patient. She was positive.

Cathy is closer to God than me. At least this is how it seems to me. She senses things in the Spirit that I don't sense. When I need help sensing something, I just ask her, and she's always right. It's a fortunate marriage for me.

When the crazy idea to become homeless first came up, Cathy was the one person I was most concerned about. *I'm not sure this is going to fly well.* But as I shared the concept with her, I was struck by how she responded. It might be, she said, "an inspired thing." I remember her saying these amazing — and, at the time, somewhat unnerving — words: "I actually feel like it could be God."

But as the days dragged on, and I was "out there," and she was "back there," she was bearing a burden all her own. *How is he doing? Where is he? How is it going?*

I found places to charge my cell phone, and we talked each day, at least for a couple minutes. I could hear a bit of the strain in her voice. She's home alone at night, she can't sleep all that well, wondering where I am. It's the *not knowing.* In some ways, maybe it was easier for me than for her, because I was in it. I wasn't wondering. I was doing it.

There was a certain irony, I guess, to her being uncomfortable, at home alone, in an empty house, because her husband was uncomfortable, *not* at home, but also alone.

But my family joined me on the journey, as much as they could. Our daughter Laine made sure our Facebook page was updated with fresh information every day. Our son Travis stayed with me on the streets a couple nights. Laine brought our grandchildren downtown to see me a couple times.

Our elder son Nate and his wife, Lisa, drove up from Los Angeles so they could spend one night with me. We went to Capitol Park the afternoon they arrived; Nate brought his guitar and played some songs in that beautiful tree-shaded setting. As he played the Johnny Cash song "Man in Black," my heart was shattered all over again. It's not legal for me to reprint the lyrics here, but I would love to. I can tell you that it talks about "the poor and the beaten down, livin' in the hopeless, hungry side of town." It also talks about those of us who are "doin' mighty fine ... in our streak of lightnin' cars and fancy clothes."

The song makes explicit its purpose: "Just so we're reminded of the ones who are held back." The perfect song, for me, for that moment.

The next morning, we walked to Loaves & Fishes. Along the way, we talked with people living along the street, people experiencing a life that most of us will never know — and never can, unless we go there with a desire to know.

Laine brought Judah and Izzy, three and five years old, to hang out with Grandpa and with Uncle Nate and Aunt Lisa. We goofed around in the park, rolled around on the grass, under the shade of trees, had a beautiful time, just goofing around. When Laine took the children home that evening, she got them ready for a bath. Five-year-old Judah wailed. "I'm not taking a bath! I'm homeless!"

The next day, when I heard the story, I realized the uncomfortable truth: *I've gone a bit too long without a shower.* I looked different from the grandfather they were accustomed to. I smelled different.

A five-year-old kid, for a few moments, was feeling what his grandpa was feeling, and wanting to identify with it. *We're in this together.*

Maybe he was learning: *There are people who aren't like me. But they're worth identifying with.*

We were, in a number of ways, going through this as a family. Home and away, clean and otherwise.

14

GOOD TIMES

When you're homeless, people don't tend to nod pleasantly in your direction or say hello, or even make eye contact. But there were moments of human connection, even compassion. Someone offered me a bottle of water. Someone else offered me a bag of nectarines! Someone gave me a $5 bill. One day I decided to see what would happen if I carried a cardboard sign at the corner of 10th and I Streets: *NEED HELP God Bless*. Within 10 minutes, I had made $25! (I donated it to the Winter Sanctuary cause.)

There were moments of joy. One evening, my wife came to visit me. I randomly crossed the path of Mayor Kevin Johnson. A couple who attend our church run a café at the corner of Cesar Chavez Park; they saw me walking by and ushered me in for a nice meal. A man who attends our church works downtown and came looking for me; he gave me $20 and a wonderful word of encouragement!

I saw a group made up of pretty obviously "church people," and headed toward them. Their leader looked at me and didn't hesitate.

"I know your dad," he said.

I was surprised to be recognized — and surprised by such a coincidence. He was pastoring a small church off of Antelope Road. "We're small, but we do our best," he said. "We're here to help."

He had grown up in the Greek Orthodox tradition. When he was a child, without Orthodox schools in the area, his parents wanted to place him in a Catholic school, but couldn't get him in. He ended up at our Capital Christian School — three decades ago. There, he began a relationship with Jesus. My father was leading the Capital Christian ministry back then. The Antelope Road pastor told me how much Glen Cole had meant to him in those years.

Ultimately, our conversation led to the obvious question: Why was I out on the streets? When I explained, the pastor's eyes grew wide: "Can you come and tell your story at my church?" he asked. They were meeting on Saturday mornings — no conflict with my own church schedule. I agreed!

Such a wonderful, seemingly random, God-planned meeting — a divine appointment!

And I did take one strange sort of break. For some years, I have served as chaplain for the Sacramento Kings NBA team, typically ministering to the players, coaches, and staff for 15 minutes or so, in the locker room area, an hour before each home game.

In the middle of my homelessness experience, there was a home game — so I went to lead a chapel service as usual.

But it wasn't exactly "as usual." It couldn't quite be. That day, I found myself expressing concern for broken people in a strange new context: the realm of celebrity athletes, millionaires.

For those 15 minutes, two worlds connected.

I've found that some of the guys are truly devoted to Christ; others are basically superstitious: They want to "get a blessing" before they go out and compete! But there are common threads linking them all. They're often misread, misunderstood. They have insecurities. They need God in their lives. They have a lot of what the world longs for — money, possessions, status — yet they still have a deep-down need for a connection to things of the spirit, things eternal.

In profound ways, a megastar sitting on a locker room bench in my chapel service that day was no different from the addled old man sitting on a bench in Cesar Chavez Park.

We are all loved by God. All offered the gift of redemption. All unworthy — yet somehow worth Jesus' life.

15

INSPIRED BY WILLIAM

William liked to talk. I liked to listen. Conversations with William were interesting, and sometimes fun.

He was tall and thin, with a beard; not the stereotype of an extreme "street person," but by no means a typical "suburban" type either. William might be described as — and I put it this way with a heart full of affection — a little "off."

When I first noticed him, it was because he was wearing a Project Church T-shirt. Project Church is a downtown ministry led by my nephew Caleb.

I pointed to the logo. "You go there?" I asked.

"Yeah," William replied. He proceeded to tell me how great Pastor Caleb was — and how his uncle pastors "a huge church out off the freeway — it's an amazing place."

Weeks later, after I had left the streets, I was invited to speak at Loaves & Fishes. William was there — so my secret was finished. We talked afterward, and before long, he turned up at Capital Christian Center.

We formed a bond. William was struggling with alcohol. He could never seem to get sober enough to secure permanent work or housing. But by God's grace, William found grace. His life changed. To this day, he attends Project

Church, or finds a ride to attend Capital Christian Center, where he's connected with opportunities to serve people in need. He's got such a servant's heart, he's appeared on the cover of our church's magazine. He lives on the fringes, and loves God, and tries to help people.

I'm glad we met, out on the streets. William is an inspiration to me.

16

THE MEDIA ARE PEOPLE TOO?

I had visits of another kind as well — from the media.

Since the whole thing began as a fundraising campaign, getting the attention of local reporters was a plus. I was going to live on the streets whether anybody in the media noticed or not; we were prepared to communicate the story exclusively through social media if necessary. I had no idea there would be so much interest from "news people." I was interviewed numerous times during my time on the streets; and I found reporters, camera operators, and photographers to be kind beyond measure. They consistently told our story with a very positive attitude and spirit. I realize that Evangelical Christianity often runs down the press. But what I realized, out on the streets, is that media people are people too. They're doing a job; so am I. God loves them, just like He loves me. I think we need to take the measure of our Christ-likeness in our characterizations of the media — and any other group, come to think of it.

17

THE PERFECT QUESTION

Y ou know the story. In Luke 10, Jesus takes the question, "Who is my neighbor?"

It's the perfect question for us today.

We've witnessed some horrific experiences on the streets of America. We've seen lives lost in terrible ways. Our hearts have been touched deeply by both racial tensions and various responses to those tensions.

In the midst of the protests after George Floyd's heart-rending death — a policeman's knee on his neck — I woke up one morning to find a social media post from our church's digital team: Blackout Tuesday. There was an organized national movement calling on people to simply post a picture of a black rectangle, and then leave the commenting up to the Black community, so that the world could simply listen. I agreed with that sentiment: Those of us from other ethnic backgrounds should be listening carefully to what's happening in the hearts of our Black brothers and sisters.

But when I saw our church's post with the hashtag #blacklivesmatter, I had a moment of panic. Some of our church family, and others, were bound to see things differently. By 6 a.m., I was reaching out to members of our ministry team. "Should we have that hashtag on our site?" It was early enough that we could pull it down before many had seen it.

Within hours, Black Lives Matter leaders were asking everyone across the country to remove the hashtag from their posts: So many had added the tag, their system was jammed; they couldn't even communicate about upcoming events. So we removed the hashtag.

I breathed a sigh of relief. I felt better. Then, almost immediately, I felt worse again. I was conscious of my own flip-flop. *What's happening here?* I asked myself. The answer was painful: I was walking in fear of people's perceptions. Walking in fear of how people in our church would feel, people I'm connected to, people I love and relate to.

One of the things I treasure in our church is our diversity. I've spoken to our church family about racial issues over the years, and I've received really positive feedback from our church's African American community — but also less positive feedback from others, who aren't feeling it the way I'm feeling it.

I struggled all week, trying to find the path forward. How do we speak love and life to people who are hurting? How do we bring our community together? How do we heal racial conflicts? How is it that we see things like the statement "Black lives matter" so differently? Why doesn't that sound good to everybody? Why can't everyone embrace it?

And Sunday was coming. I would have to preach something. Deliver some message. With thousands protesting in the streets of our nation's cities, could I just ignore it all? Wasn't there something else I could talk about?

I tried to move away from the topic. I sincerely tried. I talked to friends. I talked to my wife — if anyone could give me an answer, she could, right? But day by day, I only grew more troubled. Troubled by the idea of ruffling feathers. But also troubled by the realization that I was troubled, trying to put this subject aside. *How could it be so difficult to find common ground?*

Finally, I had no choice. This is my calling — to look into the Scriptures and reveal what I sense to be the heart of God. To lead people — *all* people — to come together around Jesus, His message, who He is. I can't shrink back from that. I wouldn't be doing my job properly.

I've often preached what Jesus preached: "Fear not." I've told our church family that we're not to be "afraid of men" when we speak the truth, and not to be afraid of the faces of people. But now I wonder what kind of faces we've been picturing. Am I picturing the faces of people in our community who don't believe like I do, don't see the world through the same lens? Can I still speak the truth?

If I hold back, I've regressed, in a way. This is not a matter of being misunderstood, and feeling hurt about it. This is a matter of *fearing* being misunderstood, and *never going there*. In which case, the opportunity to dispel misunderstandings and come together is lost.

I feel compelled to make an effort to bring us together, to bring us into common understanding — but it means taking risks. This is raw for me.

The lawyer in Luke 10 starts questioning Jesus, almost as if in a courtroom, or a classroom — "to put him to the test." His opening question: "Teacher, what shall I do to inherit eternal life?"

Jesus answers one question with two: "What is written in the law? How do you read it?"

The lawyer recites the well-known scriptural guidelines: "'Love the Lord your God with all your heart and with all your soul and with all your strength and with all your mind'; and, 'Love your neighbor as yourself.'"

"You have answered correctly," Jesus replies. "Do this and you will live."

But the lawyer is squirming a bit. The guidelines are a bit lax for him, uncomfortably inclusive. He loves God just fine, he figures; but some of those *neighbors* — well, that's a different story.

So, "desiring to justify himself," he asks his follow-up question: "And who is my neighbor?"

At which point, Jesus rolls out the now-famous parable of the Good Samaritan. The guy gets mugged, left half dead. Two upper-class religious guys, a priest and a Levite, walk by and avoid the victim; only a Samaritan — member of a despised racial minority — stops to help, not only providing immediate care but long-term provision.

So who was "a neighbor to the man who fell among the robbers?" Jesus asks.

The answer is a no-brainer. "The one who showed him mercy," the lawyer surmises.

"You go and do likewise," Jesus advises.

Of course I have to ask, where am I in this story? It's disturbing to find a priest here — the equivalent of a pastor today, which is what I am. The pastor in the story actually walks over to the other side of the road. He doesn't want to even get close. Doesn't want to concern himself with the pain.

Then comes the Levite, a servant of the house of faith — in other words, the money man. He does what the priest did.

Only the anti-hero is a hero. The hated one is the one who expresses compassion.

Loving my neighbor crosses boundaries: socio-economic, ethnic, and otherwise. In fact, there are no boundaries. Everyone is my neighbor — every human soul.

Seeing someone in need, the Samaritan doesn't stop to try to figure out the "optics," or the context: He doesn't ask, *Where did this guy come from? Does he have a local address? Driver's license? Passport? What country is he from? Does he look like me?* No. He sees a man who's hurting, and he attends to him. Provides medicine. Binds up his wounds. Takes him to a safe place. Pays for it. Arranges for extended care, to make sure the guy has a chance to get back on his feet. It's an incredible moment.

Jesus is contrasting religion with true love.

The parable of the Good Samaritan forces me to ask myself, *Am I more concerned with myself than I am with the hurting of the world? Am I trying to protect my reputation? Can I be compassionate like a Samaritan, or am I trying to stay in some image-conscious state of being?*

My prayer is that I can become the Samaritan. Not caught up with my background, where I "come from." Not caught up with how well I've done, and how I need to take care of myself. Not looking at people who haven't done as well for themselves and saying, *That's their problem.* Not classifying them according to what they did in their past that got them into their situation. Do they deserve it? Does anyone deserve to be broken like that?

Dr. Martin Luther King, Jr. looked at the story of the good Samaritan and said, "I imagine that the first question the priest and Levite asked was, 'If I stop to help this man, what will happen to me?' But by the very nature of his concern, the good Samaritan reversed the question. 'If I do not stop to help this man, what will happen to him?'"

This has to become the Christian Question: What will happen to them? What will happen to those who are hurting if I don't stop and say, "Can I help? Can I provide a way out? Can I give you a hand up? Can I help heal your wounds? What can I do?" What if I don't do anything? What will happen to the "other?"

Among the various raging debates in our culture today is the debate over systemic racism. Many people of faith are hot about the question. I don't understand the debate. A sincere study of the past 400 years of history leads us to a clear conclusion that we've built our country on systemic racism. We have progressed somewhat, perhaps, but we have not conquered this original sin of our land.

18

BLACK KIDS ARE USED TO IT

Jane Elliott taught in a small Iowa town in the 1960s. All the students in her elementary-school class were white. The morning after Dr. King was assassinated, she asked the children if they'd like to "do an object lesson." They were delighted.

Blue-eyed children wore a blue cloth draped over their shoulders; brown-eyed children wore brown cloth. Blue-eyed children sat up front in class, and got extra helpings at lunch. Certain water fountains were off-limits to brown-eyed children. Blue-eyed children enjoyed a longer recess and got to play on a new jungle gym that the brown-eyed children weren't allowed to touch.

Over the course of the day, the blue-eyed children grew strangely arrogant toward the brown-eyed children, saying distasteful things to them. The brown-eyed children grew quiet, and withdrew. On simple tests, the blue-eyed children scored higher.

The next day, Jane Elliott asked the children to write about their experiences: *How did you feel?* Their essays were so eloquent, they were printed in the local *Riceville Recorder* newspaper, on April 18, 1968, under the headline "How Discrimination Feels." The Associated Press picked up the story and ran it nationally. Johnny Carson invited Jane Elliott onto his show.

And there was an uproar — huge backlash. *The Tonight Show* was swamped with negative letters. One notorious response: "How dare you try this cruel experiment out on white children? Black children grow up accustomed to such behavior, but white children, there's no way they could possibly understand it. It's cruel to white children and it will cause them great psychological damage."

Black children are used to it. This is a practical definition of systemic racism. Racism is built into the system. It's built into the fabric of our country.

Jane Elliott went on to become an advocate for racial understanding. She conducted a simple experiment which underlines the reality. In a room full of people, she made this offer: *Every white citizen who would be happy to be treated like our society in general treats our Black citizens, please stand.* Nobody took the offer. Why not? Because white people don't want to receive the kind of treatment that Black people receive.

So the obvious question is: Why are we so willing to accept it, to allow it, for others? Why do we act like it doesn't matter?

An African American person in the U.S. today has a 400-year history. Slavery came to North America in 1619. Black people suffered years of inhumane treatment after that. Then came independence (for whites) in 1776, and in 1787 the infamous Three-Fifths clause in our Constitution: Article 1, Section 2. For purposes of representation in Congress, each enslaved Black would be counted as three-fifths of a white person. *Three-fifths of a human being.* This is our Constitution. Is racism systemic? Yes.

In 1793, Congress passed the Fugitive Slave Act, making it a federal crime to assist an enslaved person trying to escape. A white person owns you, you can't be free, and nobody can help you escape. A white person tells you what to do every day, with whom you can bunk. A white person can tear your family apart. A white person decides what your job will be, how long you'll work — in hours per day, and in total years. Nat Turner's revolt in 1831 struck fear into the hearts of whites; it was the only effective slave rebellion in U.S. history. Turner was born on a small plantation in South Hampton County, Virginia; he inherited a passionate hatred of slavery. Who wouldn't?

After the Civil War, freeing some three million enslaved people in the rebel states, the Three-Fifths clause was eradicated: The 13th Amendment freed all enslaved people in the United States; the 14th Amendment gave them full citizenship. But the 15th Amendment, granting Black men the right to vote, wasn't widely accepted or enforced. Systemic racism was so deep, so embedded, that society found other ways to keep men and women enslaved.

No white person wants to live under someone's thumb, under somebody's rule. We didn't like being told, in the coronavirus pandemic, that we couldn't meet together in our church buildings. Imagine living under this kind of rule in every detail of life, every minute of every day, for a lifetime — for generations. Complaining starts to make sense. Protesting starts to make sense. Revolt starts to make sense.

I could skip this chapter. I could have avoided this topic in my pulpit. I could pass by on the other side of the road. But there's a mugging victim in the ditch. This is the truth. I have to speak the truth.

White people imagine that the Civil War and Emancipation solved everything. But the economics were messy. Free labor no longer. Blacks won office in the South; many whites were dismayed by their loss of control — their *race's* loss of control. The Ku Klux Klan and other white protective societies sprang up: marching, burning Blacks' homes, lynching Black people, murdering Black people.

Jim Crow laws replaced slavery; they put Black citizens into indentured servitude, legally. Took voting rights away. Controlled where they could live, how they could travel. Under Jim Crow, Black children could be seized and forced into labor. To steal control is a different kind of slavery, but slavery nonetheless.

By 1885, most Southern states had laws requiring separate schools for Black and white students. By 1900, people of color were required to be separated from white people in railroad cars, depots, hotels, theaters, restaurants, barbershops, other establishments. Early in its history, the National Association for the Advancement of Colored People, the NAACP, launched a crusade against lynching; they were desperate to stop the murder of Black people. Why does the NAACP have such a bad reputation with whites today? Systemic racism. Yes, it exists.

Our world is full of victims in the ditch. Our world is also full of priests and Levites muttering "Not my thing, not my problem." *We urgently need to take on the spirit of the Samaritan. We need to take on the spirit of the minority. Of the despised. Of the outcast. Of Jesus.* We need to follow His call, and while we're loving God, *love our neighbor.*

Who is my neighbor? The white people next door? What about the Black people marching, crying out for justice, for equal opportunity — crying out *not* to be considered three-fifths of a person.

It's not enough to say "I'm okay with them protesting." A white Christian today has to speak up on behalf of our Black brothers and sisters. Because of systemic racism, we need to say, *We can't do this anymore. We can't live this way anymore. We've got to establish equality between the races.*

Of course, as a white guy, I can't really fathom what people of color have gone through, and continue to go through. But at least I can try to walk in their shoes. I can care. I can say to my Black brothers and sisters and my white brothers and sisters, "Please help me. Let's all grow. Can't we just grow a little?"

Maybe Black history isn't painfully real to white people because it's not their own. Jackie Robinson, the first Black player in Major League Baseball, was treated like an animal. Emmett Till, a 14-year-old boy tortured and murdered in 1955. Rosa Parks, declining to give up her seat on the bus. Four young Black girls killed in a 1963 church bombing in Birmingham, Alabama. Children attacked by police dogs, knocked off their feet by fire hoses. Edmund Pettus Bridge outside of Selma: 600 peaceful marchers attacked by State Troopers, the law enforcement militia of white America, wielding whips, nightsticks, tear gas.

This list goes on and on. Barack Obama, racist backlash. Tayvon Martin. Auhmad Arbery, Breonna Taylor, George Floyd.

Every white person has to wake up to this question, and make a decision: Am I the priest, the person wrapped in religion? Am I the Levite, focused on economics? Or am I the Samaritan?

We can't ignore it anymore.

Jerry Manuel is a dear friend. He grew up in Sacramento. He managed the Chicago White Sox, then the New York Mets. He's an amazing man of faith. And he's Black.

His son, Jerry Lorenzo Manuel, lives in southern California. He's a tremendous businessperson. He wanted to come north to see his parents. He pulled into Sacramento late on a Saturday night, stopped at a gas station, pulled on his pandemic-mandatory face mask, and got out the car. The woman at the counter, a middle-aged white woman, made this remark: "Every time you guys walk in here with masks on, I think we're about to get robbed."

"Quickly reminded of my Blackness," Jerry Lorenzo wrote. His notoriety hadn't followed him from southern California. He was "no longer Jerry Lorenzo, but just another Black man. The same guy I've been my whole life, dealing with the same consistent themes."

We white people need to look for racism. It exists. It's systemic. We can change it. We can grow. We can ask God for wisdom, and ask our legislators for wisdom. How can we reform our justice system, our prison system? We need to change our community. How can we improve?

NFL quarterback Drew Brees got himself into a controversy by saying "All lives matter." Talking about Colin Kaepernick, Brees said he wouldn't ever kneel for the flag. In the outcry that ensued, Brees' wife, Brittany, asked, "How could anyone who knows us or has had interactions with us think that Drew or I have a racist bone in our body?"

But this is a version of what most white people say. In white America, we can feel good about not being racist, feel good about loving one another as God loves us, feel good educating our children about the horrors of slavery and racial discrimination, feel like we're doing our part to raise our children to love, to be unbiased. We check the boxes. But soon, after talking with a number of their Black friends, Drew and Brittany Brees found their eyes opening.

"Not until this week did Drew and I realize that this is the problem," Brittany said. "We are not listening."

White America is not hearing. We're not actively looking for racial prejudice. We're going to the other side of the road.

Do Black lives matter? Why does this hit somebody the wrong way? All lives matter? *All lives can't matter until Black lives matter.*

The idea that supporting Black people means you're anti-police is a bogus argument. I have many friends in law enforcement. I pray for them and honor them. A few police officers have done harm to the reputation of the many; we need to keep the numbers in perspective. I've seen the police wrapping arms of love around our community. We as God's people need to walk side by side with people of color *and* with police officers. It's not *either-or*. It's *both-and*.

After a local Black Lives Matter march, my son Travis and I stopped to talk to a few police officers. One was sitting in his car with the window down.

"How are you doing?" I asked.

"I'm getting tired," he said.

"I get that, man," I replied. "Hang in there. We're going to get through this."

In the days after George Floyd's death, my family and I participated in a march in Sacramento, between Oak Park Community Center and Shiloh Baptist Church. As we approached the church, an agitator with a bullhorn began yelling profanities and other awful things. A few people went to him, tried to get him to stop. At one point, he came very close to my family and me: my son Travis, his wife, Melissa, and their three children — nine, six, and four years old. Someone trying to escort the agitator away from the marchers bumped into Ella, my nine-year-old granddaughter. It scared her — all the commotion, then getting bumped — and she started crying. Before either of her parents could reach down and scoop her up, two Black women stooped down, got on Ella's level, started talking to her, comforting her, and putting their arms around her.

Ella's mom and dad stood back and watched, tears streaming down their faces. On the way home, Ella reported what happened: "It made me feel safe," she said.

19

MUSLIMS ARE PEOPLE TOO?

Muslims are people too. Is this too radical?

A man named Bruce, a retired business leader, began attending our church. He wasn't with us very long, in our very diverse church culture, before he caught the spirit. He asked me if I would be interested in building bridges with the Muslim and Jewish communities. I assured him I'm open to all kinds of things. But to be honest, what I thought was, *What am I getting myself into?*

Bruce arranged for lunch with me, a local imam, and a rabbi. Imam Mohamad Aziz headed a leading mosque. Rabbi Mona Alfi heads a leading synagogue.

I figured we'd have our biggest challenges with the imam. Rabbi Mona laughed that off. "We live together in the Middle East, Arabs and Jews," she pointed out. She figured they would have the biggest challenges with the Christian!

To this day, we still occasionally get together. Along the way, we've had some adventures.

On the 15th anniversary of a terror bombing at the synagogue, the Sacramento community rallied. Rabbi Mona invited me to speak. The synagogue was full. Imam Mohamad was there.

I prepared to be an encourager, to express how grateful we were for their contributions to the community, and our commitment to standing with them against the kind of hate represented by the bombing.

All well so far.

Then the imam asked me to speak at their Ramadan event — they break the traditional fast with a huge dinner banquet attended by 500 people. I didn't agree immediately. I checked in with our church's board. They gave me a green light.

So — what to say to a Muslim crowd?

Islam is built on five "pillars." Some are similar to Christian disciplines. They pray five times a day; we have a passion for prayer. Alms, fasting, proclaiming the faith — we can relate.

A *Sacramento Bee* reporter, a member of the synagogue, attended both the synagogue and the mosque event. He liked my boundary-crossing attitude. After the Ramadan dinner, he told me he was going to write about ecumenical connections in our community. I could imagine trouble; I asked him not to. But he was committed to doing the story.

The article featured some of my comments, unfortunately out of context. The story created a stir. Some folks appreciated it, but many Christians don't like the idea of a pastor hanging out with Muslims. These folks were vocal.

But we have to pursue relationships. It's part of our mission to try to find a way to live together, to encourage each other, to support each other. No, I probably can't lead a rabbi or an imam to faith in Christ; but I can be a friend. I can let Jesus' life and light shine through me — and then leave their eternal destiny up to God. God can work through my witness however He wants.

I'm no genius. I have no clever "grand strategy" for ecumenical connection in our community. If I see an open door, if it feels like I can express Christ's love, I stumble through it.

Today, our three faith systems are talking with each other as a result of a program called Abraham's Tent of Sacramento. This multi-faith non-profit volunteer organization focused on closer connections at all levels between members of the Jewish, Christian, and Muslim faiths, mobilizing volunteer teams to perform vital community service work. It's especially important work in a time when our region is facing serious financial challenges. Abraham's Tent matched teams of volunteers with community needs — hunger, homelessness, youth, and the environment. They supported youth programs, cleaned up the riverbed, fed the homeless. No proselytizing, just an effort to serve our community.

Harmful? I don't see how.

20

SLEEPING WITH THE MAYOR

It's sometimes surprising, the people you bump into when you're on the streets as a homeless person.

Bumping into Mayor Kevin Johnson was one of those surprises.

He thanked me for what I was doing — raising funds to keep Winter Sanctuary going — and then dropped a bombshell: He wanted to spend a night with me on the streets. I was stunned, and grateful — and then I started trying to talk him out of it. He wouldn't hear of it. He was committed. I was fretting about the logistics. This was a public official, after all. Was he going to be safe?

We decided to cross the line, out of Sacramento proper — his jurisdiction — into West Sacramento. We would sleep on the Riverwalk.

We stood on the riverbank that evening, talking about race relations, and his burden for the city. We were overlooking Sacramento, with the lights of the Tower Bridge reflecting off the water. It was a beautiful sight — no indication of the hundreds of people in need. But in those hours, it was clear that Mayor Johnson's heart for the people, and his longing for people to learn to treat each other as humans, were deeply authentic.

West Sacramento's city manager got word about the mayor's plan, and a couple West Sac police sought us out. They assured us that they would keep us safe. But they discreetly made themselves invisible.

So it became a couple guys just camping out — a surreal night, in a way. We were two friends just trying to understand life, and figure how we could help people who have burdens that are difficult to bear.

We'd brought a two-man tent; I intended for the mayor to use it himself.

"No," he said with a smile, "I'm not going in there."

"This is the best spot to be," I admonished him.

"Sorry, I'm not going in there," he insisted. "Where are you sleeping?"

I pointed to the ground. "Right here."

"Me too," he replied.

He laid out his sleeping bag on the sandy bank of the river, and I laid mine next to his. We were so tired — boom! We just fell asleep.

About 4:15, I heard stirring sounds. The mayor was rolling up his sleeping bag. I just stuck my hand up toward him; he shook my hand, and without a word he went to work.

But it had not been a good night, from a sleeping standpoint. People were coming by all night long. A couple of my team members had arranged to stand by, awake, all night long, in hopes that the mayor and I could actually get some sleep. But there's still a certain tension, sleeping outdoors in an urban setting. I didn't prefer the waterfront, even though it might seem somewhat glamorous. It just didn't feel good. I had become a homeless person: *The alley felt better to me.*

One might expect an elected official, a politician, to look for the PR angle, the photo opp, and then bug out. But Mayor Kevin Johnson was not an ordinary politician.

Some time after I had left the streets and returned to my "regular" life and ministry, I had an accident at home — trimming a backyard tree, falling from a ladder, fracturing my skull and collarbone. I spent five days in ICU and came away with temporary paralysis in my face, plus hearing loss in one ear. During my recuperation, I was homebound for quite a while. Kevin showed up, unannounced, at my house — with no media, no public attention — to check on me. If he wasn't genuine, he was a brilliant actor. Maybe politicians are people too.

I couldn't help but remember his invitation to me, some years earlier, to speak to an issue at a City Council meeting. After the meeting, he led me up to his fourth-floor office for a staff debriefing. Then, before dismissing everyone, he asked me to pray for his team.

I grinned awkward. "Is this legal?" I asked. I was having a church-state separation crisis moment. He urged me to go ahead, and I did.

I have wrestled with my prejudices about people of influence, power, and wealth. And I have come to a place of hoping this for them: that they will come to see the extraordinary blessings God has bestowed upon them as a *calling*, and use their leadership position as a means of impacting the world. I admire the wealthiest people who have signed on to the giving challenge, pledging to give enormous portions of their money to world-changing causes. Some of their choices wouldn't be my choices, but I'm grateful that some have chosen to use their wealth to alter the lives of people in need. *Everyone can change somebody's world.* The ultra-wealthy simply have the potential to make much more of a change in more people's lives than you or I could. When a wealthy person develops a heart for people in need and gives to help them — and then looks around and asks, *What more can I do?* — that's a good thing. My prayer for the wealthy is that they learn to look beyond the money; that they come to realize they are not defined by their money, but by *who they are.*

My experiences with the difficult issues of our day have led me to a simple but effective goal: to move past the political, to the pastoral. The political view is that Mr. X is worth his money, and Mr. Y is worth his fame, and Mr. Z is worth his status. But the pastoral view is: *How can one person influence others, and change their lives for the better?*

Likewise, at the bottom end of the social spectrum — on the street, among the homeless and the hopeless — can I look at someone *not* as a problem, *not* as a political or economic issue, but as a human being in need of God's love and care? I have to see them differently before I can bring change into their lives. A new vision of people will be the beginning of the process of changing them. The first step isn't changing them. The first step is changing me.

Which is what happened to me when I "descended to the streets" and became homeless.

21

FLASHBACK

People can change, if we change how we see them.

One night, preparing to sleep outdoors, I walked along with my companion toward our intended overnight spot. Suddenly he stopped. He looked around. To me, it was an utterly ordinary inner-city alley.

"I lived here," he said, "for about eight months."

He unfolded his story. Six years earlier, he was an alcoholic. He drank himself into losing his job, burning his bridges with his family. He had nowhere to go.

"I walked this alley," he said, "and others."

His eyes were moving over the landscape of concrete, asphalt, brick, and stone.

"I just had a flashback of my old life," he said quietly.

He eventually found his way off the streets through the Salvation Army's rehab program. He got his life on track. He lives a life of sobriety now. He's married. He has a very responsible job. He's doing life in a beautiful way. He was with me that night because he wanted to give back, to find a way to serve, to help others.

Change is doable. There is hope. It is possible to make a difference in somebody's life.

22

WHAT TO BE THANKFUL FOR

So many blessings, and so many of them taken for granted.

That's my life.

I am thankful for a car. As a homeless person, I walked an average of 14,000 steps a day. One day, 18,000 steps. A lot.

I am thankful for a house to go home to. Learning to be a homeless person, searching for a place to sleep, I tried a parking garage. It seemed perfect — till a security officer arrived and ran me off. I wandered until I found a park, a little elevated from the level of the street. It was about 10 p.m. I laid my sleeping bag on the concrete under the night sky. This worked beautifully for three nights — although concrete makes a hard bed. I tossed and turned.

On the fourth night, I arrived before dark and laid my bag out. Five minutes later, two officers road up on bicycles and let me know I couldn't stay there. Technically, it's a state park. "We have to make sure everyone is out by dark," one officer said.

It occurred to me I could try City Hall. Sacramento had enacted an ordinance to keep the homeless from camping out in the city; but a big protest ensued, with people setting up tents at City Hall, and the City Council had backed off on enforcement. Hope! I made my way there and laid my bag out with about 20 other people. (The next morning, I searched for an available restroom in City Hall.)

The next night, rain was predicted, so City Hall was out. I found an office building with covered walkways. I scouted it out in daylight, hoping no one would be patrolling that area. It rained through the night, but I was able to stay dry.

The next day, no rain was predicted, but it rained anyway. All the homeless people were scrambling for shelter. I found a shopping area with a covering. It rained all night, but I didn't get rained on at all. Success! But I saw others sleeping outside my lucky place — they were drenched.

I learned that the officers roll into the park around 8 p.m. So I arrived at 9.

On the streets, I learned to be thankful.

I always thought of myself as a thankful person, but thankfulness takes on a new intensity when you don't have your usual stuff.

When I'm thankful for everything, for every little blessing, I'm not as critical. Thankfulness makes me kind. It makes me more humble. I lose my spirit of entitlement. With the attitude of "This is mine," I'm destructive. But when I see everything I have as a gift, I become more of an encourager, less of a critic.

I tried to preach about this, but I realized I had become critical of critics. What's up with this? The critical people make me critical? *I must return to thankfulness.*

I am thankful for a mattress. I have spent restless nights on concrete. You start to realize how the will to improve one's situation is drained out of a person when you're sleep deprived and on your own to survive. I had the choice to go home. Others on the street don't have such a choice. I had a cell phone. Every night, I woke up every 60 to 90 minutes, checked my phone, tried to go back to sleep. One night, the third time I awoke, I realized I'd been dreaming that the leaders of Capital Christian Center were asking me to leave the church.

Even just seven nights on the streets wear you down. I was tired. I started feeling stripped of how to think right. Seven nights. How do you do this if you have to do it for seven months? Even if someone shows you a path through, it might be a struggle to grab hold of hope. The street strips you of the strength to believe that it might be possible to navigate life.

I am thankful for restrooms. On the street, I learned where I could find public facilities. They were rarely accessible to me in the morning. I found bushes.

I am thankful for a shower. And so are the people around me.

I am thankful for a sound mind. I came away from the streets with a heart heavy for those who are mentally or emotionally disturbed. I did find that there is room in my heart to love them, instead of dismissing them as if they have no value.

I am thankful for friends who love me. Not just those who came out to sleep on concrete with me, although I am deeply grateful to them. But I am also thankful for the many words of encouragement I received, personally and virtually, while I was on the street. I bumped into a couple who attend our church and work at a restaurant just across from Cesar Chavez Park; they bought me lunch at their restaurant and showed me much love and encouragement. Walking through Capitol Park, I came upon a small group of people setting up for a concert. The leader explained the outreach, then offered me food prepared for his team. I was chased down by a young couple whose wedding I had conducted a year earlier; they offered to buy food, either for me to consume or for me to give away to others.

I am thankful for the Catholic Order of the Sisters of Mercy. Walking through the Capitol grounds, I came across a statue of two sisters helping a child. The inscription says they began their ministry during the Gold Rush years, helping sick and orphaned children.

I am thankful for Sister Libby, a modern-day sister of mercy who rides a bicycle with supplies on her back to help the hurting of our community one person at a time.

I am thankful for my family and their love for me. Cathy graced me with affirmation that she could sense this whole "homelessness thing" was right for me to do. My daughter Laine came downtown with our outreach team providing 50 pairs of new running shoes donated by Fleet Feet for us to give away. My sons Nate and Travis, the list goes on.

I am thankful for Jesus. I felt His presence with me on the streets. I know He loves each of the broken people I saw there, just as much as He loves me. He never gives up on anyone.

Not even me, when I'm off track.

23

GOD'S DIFFERENT IDEA

There are great novels, and some of them aren't fiction. One of the greatest stories of all time is found in the Old Testament. It starts at about chapter 38 of the book of Genesis, and goes all the way through chapter 50.

By chapter 40, Joseph is laboring in prison, but somehow, mysteriously, miraculously, everything Joseph does ends up going well. Even in prison, he winds up being the leader of the inmates.

Then two new inmates arrive: the king's cupbearer and baker. The cupbearer tastes the king's drinks in advance to make sure they're not poisoned. I'm not sure whether the baker had to pre-taste the bread for poison too. But somehow, both guys get in trouble with the king and end up in prison. With Joseph.

There, both guys have confusing dreams. Joseph is a dreamer from way back; he knows how to sense what God is saying through dreams. The cupbearer describes his dream; Joseph says, in essence: Three days from now, Pharaoh will restore you to your old position. *Remember me,* he says to the cupbearer. *Get me out of prison.* Joseph was tired of prison. He was ready to be free.

The baker brings his dream to Joseph too. Joseph tells the truth. Three days, and Pharaoh will execute you.

It all happens, as predicted. The cupbearer goes back to work; the baker is hanged.

But the cupbearer doesn't remember Joseph. Joseph is sitting in prison, hearing the news: baker dead, cupbearer redeemed. Joseph has to be wondering: *When will things turn for me? When do I get out of the pit? The cupbearer got his miracle. When do I get mine?*

Joseph's prison story is our story. We develop our agenda. It's in our mind. We envision everything happening in a way that seems rational to us. *This is the way it should be.* But then things don't happen according to our agenda.

Joseph doesn't just have a bad day. Joseph has a bad decade. He's stuck in this prison for 10 years.

Sometimes God's promises don't unfold the way we expect them to. The delays, the challenges. What in the world is going on? Why are things the way they are?

At which point: Do I keep listening to God, hoping in Him? Or some other source?

Our world is noisy. A lot of voices compete for our attention. I don't know these voices' character. I don't know their motivation. But as I put my hope in God as my source, He will put the right people around me, to guide me onto the path that I should follow.

Isaiah 55:6 says: "Seek the Lord while he may be found; call upon him while he is near." He's not distant. He's not off somewhere, busy with something else. He's with us. We can tune in.

And we need to, because God's thoughts aren't ours. His are better, higher. He knows things we don't know. I'm going to put my hope in Him. I can rest assured that He's going to show me the way.

Some won't travel the road I'm traveling, or even at the same pace I'm traveling it. This isn't cause for hostilities. I need to keep the door open to people who aren't following the same path as me right now. Maybe tomorrow, they will. Let them. I can't stand against them, in judgment against them. My role is to keep the door open, pray for them, and let the Holy Spirit do whatever work is to be done in their hearts. And mine.

God's ways are above our ways. His thoughts are above my thoughts. He's doing something, but maybe I don't fully understand it. Maybe I don't like my circumstances at the moment.

What is my pit, my prison? Am I there unjustly?

We live in a culture of rights. I have rights. I insist on my rights. You have no right to deprive me of my *rights*. It isn't right.

When I envision my agenda, it can become a checklist of entitlements.

But God's ways are different. He has a different plan. In His view, *my responsibilities are greater than my rights.* I have a responsibility to love, and serve, and pray. I have a responsibility to wrap my arms around people in need. I have responsibilities far more important than my rights.

And as I pursue my responsibilities, rather than my rights, God protects me, provides for me. Even when, like Joseph, I'm spurned or even forgotten.

In the astonishing novel of Joseph's life, 13 years go by. He's now the vice president of Egypt. The world is wracked by famine. His own family, back in Israel, is at risk of starvation. But Joseph, tuning in to God's guidance, has wisely set up a huge system to guarantee a food supply.

In this moment, Joseph realizes that everything he's been through — abandonment by his brothers, enslavement, false accusation, prison — it was all for a purpose: to save his family, and multitudes of others.

Today, we might say we're living in a time of imprisonment. A "moment of the pit." What does God call us to do? We may not be able to figure out what He's doing, but there's a reason we're going through this. We need to keep trusting God. Hoping in God. Tuning in to God. And we know this: He will not call us to fear, or hatred, or selfishness. He will call us to courage, and kindness, and generosity.

The dream God gives me is not just for me; it is for the salvation of others. When I'm obedient to Him — when I follow Him, not cutting corners for my own comfort — He uses me for the good of others, for the good of the community. He's called us to serve.

In our day, many have come to think of ranting as the best way to help people. This is a delusion. Better to pray — and let God work. Better to find ways to help, and trust Him to move in areas where we can't. He will use us to bring about His purposes in the earth.

Jeremiah 29:11-13 is not just a comforting series of slogans. It is practical guidance: "For I know the plans I have for you, declares the Lord, plans for welfare and not for evil, to give you a future and a hope. Then you will call upon me and come and pray to me, and I will hear you. You will seek me and find me, when you seek me with all your heart."

In the natural, my heart gets distracted. My mind and my mouth are working too many angles. I'm endlessly trying to figure out what other people's jobs should be, and how they should be doing them. I've got all the answers. I'm a brilliant armchair quarterback, sitting in my easy chair — without even a football — insisting that I know best. I'm missing Jeremiah 29. I need to turn to God. He has plans for us. He's going to prosper us, not harm us. He will give us a future and a hope. But we need to seek Him with all of our heart.

This world is divided. Our country is divided. Too many are against one another. Let it not be the believers that turn against the unbelievers. This cannot be our position. *We are for them.* I am *for* every lost soul, that they might come to know who Jesus is. How are we going to help them if we're ranting at them? Let them come. Don't berate them, don't criticize them; let them come, because we're praying that the Spirit of the living God will fall upon the land when we seek Him with all our heart.

24
RANTING

I don't always take my own advice. I don't always listen to my own preaching.

I have been known to rant.

Living on the streets will bring out the "rant" in a guy.

Hanging around Cesar Chavez Park, with its ever-morphing population of homeless people, I heard a few rants. Someone will suddenly start yelling; you look to see what's going on. It can be the ramp-up of a fight. Or it can be someone taking issue with an imaginary friend. It can go on and on; or it can surge and just as quickly fade.

Some days, I felt a bit crazy. But I hadn't started yelling in the park. At least not yet.

Then it happened.

It was 8 a.m., and a city worker with a noisy leaf-blower was clearing the sidewalk, but sending the dirt and junk into the air and onto "my" bench. I dodged the cloud of dirt and dust — and I guess something snapped in me. I motioned to the worker; he pulled off his headphones, and I started yelling at him.

"Man, what are you doing? This bench is filthy dirty now!"

He clearly wasn't happy. He started walking away, and threw a line over his shoulder: "Why don't you just go home."

"Home!" I exploded. "This is my home! I'm homeless!"

I pointed to the bench. "That's my couch! And you got it all dirty! *Go blow off my couch!*"

He didn't.

But in my heart, I thought, *That was kind of fun.* Sleeping outdoors, on concrete, beats you down, physically and emotionally. You get ragged. You feel on edge. Now, here, I was experiencing a kind of release.

But overnight, I felt bad.

The next day, I saw the same city worker. Awash in remorse, I approached him again.

"Hey man, I yelled at you yesterday. I've felt bad about it ever since. That was wrong for me to do, and I'm sorry."

He waved me off with half a smile. "Ah, forget about it," he said. "It happens to me all the time."

"Well, it shouldn't have happened from me," I replied, "and I'm sorry."

He shrugged. There was nothing more to be said or done. Twin errors — "Go home" and an outburst of rage. Our world in miniature.

America has been torn by racial unrest and rocked by protests. Many are saying, or secretly thinking, "Can't we just get past this and move on to something else?" But avoidance can be dangerous. In terms of race relations, "getting past this" has been done many times. Clearly, the issue hasn't gone away. We as Christians need to stay in this conversation.

We have a tendency to think in terms of "learning the Bible," as if it's a finite process; you get to the destination and you've learned it all. But we are called by God to be *lifelong learners*, always growing, always striving to become the best version of ourselves. And part of this learning and growing process involves hearing different perspectives, digesting them, factoring them in to what we've already learned. *Shutting out alternative perspectives shuts down our own growth.*

Much of today's public conversation about race relations is very divided and divisive, pitting one way of thinking against another, or one people group against another. Until we make it a conversation, with equal parts speaking and *listening*, instead of simply a shouting match, there will be no progress.

Diversity is reality. We should embrace it. We can't pretend it doesn't exist, and it's unhealthy to fight it. Jesus chose His disciples from a variety of backgrounds, from the fisherman to the tax collector, and a variety of personalities. When they came together to follow Jesus, they didn't lose their identities. When their opinions differed, they had to work through them — and ultimately turn to Jesus.

Likewise, when we disagree, we have to work through those disagreements. We have to engage in conversation — in the context of our loyalty to Jesus.

The best friends, the most valuable friendships, are marked by a freedom to raise difficult issues, a sense of safety in addressing disagreements. *What you said, that hurt me. Where was that coming from?* This kind of give and take deepens each party's understanding of the other. Our journey together grows richer.

The person I don't understand, or with whom I disagree, is just as fearfully and wonderfully made as I am. I'm not God's only child. I can disagree with you or be puzzled by you and still honor you as God's creation.

And I can listen. I can ask God, "Is this truth?" God will confirm His Word in our hearts. I don't have to fear error. Nobody has to defend truth. Truth defends itself.

In America, everyone has a right to publicly protest, to outwardly share their opinions, their dissatisfaction. Jesus was a major protester! He didn't go along with the norms of the day. He was ridiculed, ostracized, and demonized because of his protests. His views went against the elite. He went against the grain.

Protest is in our spiritual DNA. As Christians, we're called to be bold, to confront injustice and unrighteousness, to speak out in defense of those who are being marginalized, disenfranchised. *The motive of Christ's protests was compassion. The motive of our protests must be compassion.*

Jesus protested mistreatment; he aligned Himself with those who were despised because of their ethnicity, and He healed the sick. Today, we are called to act justly, love mercy, and walk humbly with our God. We are called to do the right thing for people.

Some white people feel they're being asked to take responsibility for injustices that happened decades or even centuries ago. *Why should I feel guilty for being white?* But this question misses the point of today's protest movement. We all experience pain in life. But my white skin is not what has contributed to my pain. White skin isn't a mark against me. A Black person's skin, on the other hand, puts them at a disadvantage that I don't experience. I've never been treated differently just because I'm white.

I had no say in which family I was born into. I have white privilege through no fault of my own. But in our racist system, I get to take advantage of white privilege because the system was created and designed for whites. Nothing in the system was created for Black, indigenous, and people of color. They're the ones getting the crumbs from the table.

There is systemic racism, and the system needs to be addressed. How do we fix it? This is the great cultural question.

I marched in Sacramento, along with our chief of police. I considered it a privilege. I was there representing who we are in Christ. Not because of politics. Not because I'm an activist. I marched to call for an end to racism, injustice, marginalization of minorities. I marched in favor of better programs for the homeless, better housing for those who need it. "Justice for everyone." It's what Jesus stood for.

It is appropriate for a white Christian to say, "Help me understand white privilege, and how I can be a better person, how I can partner with others in my community to advance the cause of justice. I'll never be able to walk in a Black person's shoes, but if I have relationship with you, I can learn, and grow, and move into a more effective role."

Jesus paid a dear price for His protests. He died at Calvary. He didn't hang on a cross for the whites and then go back later to hang on a cross for Blacks. He died one death for all ethnicities. He calls us *all* to talk in love, in humility, in respect, in understanding.

Some things need to change. What are the next steps? What adjustments need to be made in government, in policing, in education?

We are responsible. We live in a democracy, which means we have a say. We must do our part. We must hold ourselves accountable.

In the Old Testament, David messed up. Then he acknowledged his sin and asked God to give him a clean heart, a right spirit. If I have a heart of fear or hatred or apathy toward someone who doesn't look like me, *I'm messed up.* I need to acknowledge my sin, and ask God to give me a clean heart, a right spirit. Many of my white friends today haven't gotten to the point of saying "I'm messed up." They haven't confronted their inner fear or hatred or apathy toward people of color. They don't feel they need a clean heart or a right spirit. They think they're already clean and right. They're wrong.

We need to recognize the heart of Jesus for people who are hurting and develop the same kind of heart. We need to see people differently and respond to people differently than we have been.

Until we do, we can't share the "Good News." We can't represent Christ to our world. We can't be effective in "evangelism" or "discipleship" or any of the other functions on which we've traditionally placed such great value. We have to start by admitting we have a problem. We have to want to become part of the solution, first by *changing ourselves.*

25

CHOOSING THE POOR

How much like Jesus do I look?

When the world looks at me, how much of Jesus do they see?

These are good questions to keep asking. *God, how do I think like you? How do I love like you? In this broken world, this place of turmoil, how can I represent you best?*

The apostle James, in the second chapter of his epistle, urges us to "show no partiality." No special treatment for the guy with the nice jewelry and expensive suit, as opposed to the guy in the shabby clothes.

"Has not God chosen those who are poor in the world to be rich in faith and heirs of the kingdom?" James writes. "Love your neighbor as yourself," he continues. "If you show partiality, you are committing sin."

Oppression of the poor has been part of the human scene since the beginning of time. There's something inherent in our depravity, in the fallen nature of man, that seeks status and then lords it over those lower down on the ladder.

But the Scripture shows us that God actually *chooses* the poor. If we follow God, we must likewise choose the poor. How can we choose the poor? We can learn.

Earlier in his letter, James writes, "Let the lowly brother boast in his exaltation." Jesus lifts us up out of our lowliness. God's Word reveals here that He is for *all* people. He levels the playing field for everyone. We tend to look at the world in a natural way, missing the spiritual reality: *We are all lowly in spirit.* We are all depraved. We don't have goodness within that can save us. Each of us is broken. I have sin. I fall short of the glory of God. But in the natural world, we see people differently. Some folks haven't found their way, some are stuck, some live in poverty, some are troubled and hurting — and I see myself as better. But God says, "I've come to liberate the poor. They can boast in their exaltation."

My tendency is to say *I did this, look what I did. I've found my way. I've got my position. I've got my power. I have my riches.* And I look down on those who haven't found their way to my level. But in the same passage of Scripture, where God says the lowly should boast in their exaltation, He says the rich should boast in their humiliation!

I grapple with this. We so automatically think we've achieved our successes on our own. *I excelled through my intellect, my talents. I'm self-made.* We take credit for what we've accomplished. But they're all gifts from God. I can't boast in my possessions, my power, my money. I can only boast in Jesus' power, in the fact that I can't save myself, but that I have a Savior.

If someone doesn't have what I have, I have no call to see myself as somehow superior. I'm not called to draw barriers around your neighborhood and mine to try to keep you *in* yours and *out* of mine. I'm called to erase the barriers, to set aside the partiality. It's not about what you have, or what you look like. God erases the barriers and the boundaries and gives us all the same heart. It's what I have in the spiritual realm that gets me where I need to go. We can come together in a beautiful way on common ground. Knowing that humans tend to be partial, the biblical God levels the playing field by *choosing* the poor and the oppressed.

Paul writes in 1 Corinthians 1:27-28, "God chose what is foolish in the world to shame the wise; God chose what is weak in the world to shame the strong; God chose what is low and despised in the world, even things that are not, to bring to nothing things that are." God chose. God chose. God chose. God chose the poor. God chose the lowly. So that no human being might boast in the presence of God. *Let the one who boasts boast in the Lord.*

Most of the people who came to faith in the early days of the Church were poor. They've been oppressed. Jesus' message of liberation through His death and resurrection is coming to people who were struggling. They're meeting together house to house.

They're sharing bread with each other. They're taking care of one another. They're selling what they can to provide for a brother. They're coming from a place of poverty.

Search history and you find that the message of Jesus thrives in places of poverty. We see huge numbers of Jesus-followers in countries of greater poverty. The message of liberation, the message of exaltation, gives hope! It's a life-giving message for a person who feels oppressed and wonders what the future holds. Jesus liberates the broken, the troubled. Faith is harder for those who have more.

I don't have any goodness to bring to God. It's only because of Him that goodness can flow through me. He can change me to do good works.

The secular world declares that you get what you can grab, go for it, own it, rule it — and then life's over. (You plan a cool vacation. You look forward to it. You keep thinking about it, envisioning it. You're eager. Then, *bam* — it's over.) Jesus offers a different plan: liberation, freedom from sin, *eternal life.*

Jesus offers dignity to everyone. The poor can be elevated. *Blessed are the poor in spirit.* Theirs is the kingdom of heaven! That's who I want to be: considering myself poor in what I need, and unable to earn it. Unable to get out of my debt. Poor in spirit. I can only be exalted by His grace — and I will celebrate that!

If I assume a "rich guy" mentality, and look down on those who haven't acquired as much as I have, and assume they're oppressed because they somehow manufactured their own oppression — they're responsible for the mess they've gotten themselves into — I'm missing the truth about *myself.* We are all sinners. We all come to Jesus via the same path.

Jesus nails this concept when He talks to the Pharisees, the religious leaders of His day. (As a member of the clergy, I'm concerned about adopting the same views and behaviors as those guys.) In Matthew 21:31, He advises them, "The tax collectors and the prostitutes go into the kingdom of God before you." This had to be unsettling to the clergy! Tax collectors were extortionists, thieves. And prostitutes!

But Jesus goes on to remind them that John the Baptist had proclaimed the truth, and it was the "sinners" who believed him — not the religious types. You and I need to believe the way they believed: believe we need Jesus; believe we're broken. The lowly ones latched on to hope through Jesus because they saw that this was their only hope for getting out of the difficult spot they were in. But the religious leaders, who were following the letter of the law — crossing the Ts, dotting the *Is, I did this, I did that* — they couldn't see themselves as broken. They couldn't see themselves as needing Jesus the way the tax collectors and prostitutes did. They were missing the boat. The tax collectors and prostitutes were going to get into heaven ahead of them.

95

In the synagogue, in Luke 4, Jesus reads aloud the prophecy of Isaiah: "The Spirit of the Lord is upon me, because he has anointed me to proclaim good news to the poor ... to set at liberty those who are oppressed ..."

Not to the successful. Not to the glamorous. To the losers.

We can get so churched that we think we've got it all figured out. We think in terms of *all those people out there.* We develop a kind of separation between the churched world and the secular world, as if *all those people* are our enemies. *They are all precious to God.* They are objects of God's affection — and should be of ours too.

If God chooses the poor, we must also choose the poor. We must see how precious they are and help those in need. If I have a clear, definite connection to God, I'll take on His heart. I'll take on His spirit.

Martin Luther summarized faith and works with this statement: "Christians are saved by faith alone, but not by faith which remains alone." Once we come to faith, our faith motivates us to do works. The works don't save us. Faith in Jesus, in His finished work, is what saves us — and that alone. But once we are saved, we have the joy of getting in the game! We get to be a part of His plan. Good works are not a means of salvation. They are a sign of salvation. They reveal what team we're on. They reveal to whom we belong.

How do you know you're resting in the saving grace of Jesus? The sign of a person who knows they are a sinner saved by grace is *their care for the poor* — because Jesus chose to come and help the poor. The oppressed. To set at liberty the captive. To lift up those who are put down, pushed down, held down. His heart is drawn to them so much. When we find our pathway of faith, then we are compelled inevitably to do the same: to have a heart for the broken, for the oppressed.

Yeah, but what if it's really their fault that they're in such a state?

James writes, "For judgment is without mercy to one who has shown no mercy. Mercy triumphs over judgment" (James 2:13). If I shoot darts at people who are broken, people who haven't yet found the pathway of faith in Jesus, what happens to *me?* I judge, and judge, and judge — I'm not showing mercy to broken people, where there's a need for it. People who have everything all together, what do they need my mercy for? They're fine. But people who are broken, people who are struggling, people who are in a hard place, need mercy: God's mercy, and the mercy of my heart.

When I look at the world we're in right now, this is what touches me. I feel drawn to mercy. But I hear a different sound coming from religious quarters: negativity, judgmentalism. It sounds like war. My head starts spinning. There are people who have great needs right now, people who are broken, people crying out for someone to lift the oppression off of their souls. They're clamoring for help. Yet all we offer in response is judgment?

I don't want to stand before God in that state of being. Because judgment shows no mercy for those who have not shown mercy. I'm going to be judged terribly.

I didn't figure this out on my own. Jesus came and rescued me, on the streets. Because he has rescued me, I have a heart for those who aren't yet rescued. I have a heart to choose the poor and oppressed. I have a heart to say, "How can I help you? What can I do right now?"

Our world is massively broken. We the Church should be able to go into the midst of the heartbreak and say, "I want to hear what's in your heart. I want to hear what's tearing you apart. How can I help? How can I heal? What can I do to lift you up? What can I do to wrap my arms around you? I want to show mercy. I don't want to show judgment." Mercy triumphs over judgment.

Back to Jesus' story of the Good Samaritan: the mugging victim, the religious guys who avoid the problem, the member of a despised racial minority who helped. "Who was the good neighbor?" Jesus asks. Answer: *the one who showed him mercy.* "Do likewise," Jesus says — not only to His audience that day, but to us, today.

The Black community today is broken. There are myriad reasons and causes. But instead of standing back as a white religious leader and judging what it's all about, I feel broken. I have no right to speak any kind of judgment. Judgment is not Jesus. Judgment is not what He's called me to do. He says to the oppressed, "Boast in your exaltation." He says to the privileged, "Boast in your humiliation."

This isn't cause for guilty feelings. My guilt has already been removed. I am not feeling the guilt of my past, or of my present. I am saved, I am forgiven. But I feel the humiliation of needing that grace. I am feeling keenly the fact that without that grace, I'm lost. Without that grace, there's no hope. I can't feel elevated over anyone. I can only feel drawn to those who are crying out. I want to go stand with those who are broken. I want to listen to what they have to say. I don't want to evaluate it, and pick it apart, and decide what's real and what's not. What's real is our brokenness. What's real is Jesus choosing the poor and the oppressed. It's what He was anointed for.

When we come to faith in Jesus, we simultaneously hold two positions. In myself, I'm a sinner condemned, deserving punishment. But in Christ, I'm absolutely loved, and absolutely accepted, and absolutely liberated. I can't forget what I was — can't forget that without Jesus there's no hope for me. I have to remember what I am, that He has set me free. Which helps me look at those around me and say, "I'm just like you. And I have some hope to offer you. I have a message that can liberate you. I have a message that can give you victory."

We must learn to choose the poor. "He who has ears to hear, let him hear." Are we listening? Is our spirit open? Are we seeking this truth?

Jesus died at the hands of injustice, yet preached His good news to the poor. We need to get this in our hearts. "Show no partiality." Jesus was lifted up on the cross to draw all people to Himself (John 12:32). He wasn't pretty hanging there. He was torn up, disfigured, humiliated, lowly. It wasn't a secular brand of beauty that drew people to Him. Jesus demonstrated beauty through brokenness. Beauty through humiliation. Beauty through suffering. It's almost as though He was saying, "I will give up all my beauty in order to make you beautiful. I will become ugly so that you can receive the only beauty that really lasts." The beauty that chooses the broken. The beauty that says, "How can I help?"

How can we choose the poor? In our church, we stage food giveaways. Those who can't serve can donate funds. Many of our members volunteer with various charities in the Sacramento community. Some sponsor children from families who can't afford tuition to our Christian school. Some support other inner-city schools in various ways. The list goes on.

We are trying to learn to choose the poor.

26

"WON'T BE TOO LONG"

The day finally came. It was time to go home.

I planned to catch the light rail Saturday at 5 p.m. I spent the afternoon in the library, preparing my remarks for the services at church that evening and the following morning. By 4, I was ready, so I took a final stroll through Cesar Chavez Park on my way to the train.

A church group had just arrived, giving away food. I hadn't eaten all day. I hurried to get in line with all the rest of the homeless.

A woman got in line behind me. I struck up a conversation. She talked about her nighttime routine. "I find a spot in a doorway, sometimes a bench," she said. "But I have to keep moving, because they don't want you in certain places. You have to keep on the move."

She'd been on the streets for four months. But she was looking ahead.

"It won't be too long and my daughter is coming back," she reported. "I'm going to get off the street hopefully in about a month."

"That's awesome!" I replied. "Where's your daughter coming from?"

"Well, she's in jail," she answered. "She's getting out in about 30 days."

"Sweet!" I said. "Does she have a place?"

"No," her mother answered, "but she has the ability to make an income. So we're going to get together. We're going to get it worked out. She's going to help me."

I headed back to the church, but my spirit was still in the park. I couldn't get the woman's face out of my mind. She was the last picture from my journey. The last story. Sleeping in doorways, dodging the cops, waiting for a daughter to get out of jail. A tale of troubles. Unique, yet typical.

I came back to the life I love, but I couldn't shake her face. I can still see her — and so many others: the faces of people sunk deep in despair, yet people whose souls have value. There's a light behind the darkness.

God comes into the darkness. He doesn't bark at us and tell us to get it together. He says, "I'm coming to rescue you. I'm coming to help you. I'm coming to take the darkness away from you. And leave a little bit of light behind me."

To see that light — that's the challenge for the rest of us.

27

MISSING JESUS

J esus incarnated into our lives to understand us, to care about us. It wasn't for Him, it was for others. This is the spirit of Christ, the spirit we are called to model in our world. We are called to be Jesus incarnate here, so we can understand the pain of the homeless person, the struggles of the addicted person, the battles of the oppressed, the pressures of minorities.

Being incarnate in the world means looking at people through a different lens, empathizing with someone else's experience. It's difficult in the world we're in, trying to put ourselves into someone else's shoes and still advocate for righteousness and for godliness. But we are up to the challenge, because of Jesus. He has shown us the way, how to live for the other. And now He's calling us to do the same.

In John 20, after Christ's crucifixion, several of His followers go to the tomb and find it empty. They're confused. They still haven't embraced the idea that Jesus has risen. "Who took Him?" They're not sure what happened yet. Befuddled, the disciples head home.

But then there's Mary Magdalene. After the others depart, she's weeping outside the tomb. But when she stoops to look into it, she sees two angels in white sitting where the body of Jesus was, one at the head, one at the feet.

"Woman, why are you weeping?"

She tells them why — someone has taken Jesus away, she has no idea where — then she turns and sees Jesus standing there. But she doesn't recognize Him.

He repeats the angels' question: "Woman, why are you weeping? Whom are you seeking?"

Mary figures He's the gardener. She starts negotiating for the missing body.

Finally, He speaks her name. Suddenly, the light dawns for her. She calls Him Teacher. She wants to hug Him. Instead, He sends her to tell the guys.

She goes. "I have seen the Lord," she reports. It's an eyewitness account.

Mary Magdalene is the first person to see Jesus after His resurrection.

There's something very significant and powerful about this. Mary Magdalene is a member of Jesus' ministry team. There was a time when she wasn't in her right mind; Jesus cast seven demons out of her. Since then, she's been part of a group of women who traveled and helped serve Jesus in His ministry.

She's from Magdala, a town on the western shore of the Sea of Galilee. Today, Magdala is being excavated. It was a resort city, filled with activity — and immorality. All kinds of people came through. There was a thriving prostitution industry. Mary may have been one of those sex workers. Jesus set her free from all that. He revolutionized her.

Yet she and the others missed so many clues! An empty tomb? He had said He would rise again. But of course, resurrection is a hard idea to grasp. The graveclothes lying there — another clue. If somebody stole the body, why didn't they take Him in His clothes? Missed clue.

Angels, dressed in white, sitting where the body had been. Pretty good clue. To the others, the angels had to say, "Don't be afraid." Mary is stronger. She sees them and strikes up a conversation.

But she still misses the moment.

Why didn't she recognize Him, when she finally saw Him? Maybe He'd been so brutalized by the torture and the crucifixion, He was disfigured beyond identification. But now — resurrected and beautiful, a picture of perfection — He wasn't what she expected.

It's still true today. Millions of people are missing who Jesus is. So many clues, He's right there — but He's not what people expect. Mary, even as committed as she was to Him, still needed a moment of revelation in order to make the connection. She needed the gift of faith. So do we.

In our world of turmoil, with all the confusion the enemy brings, it's easy to miss Jesus. But I can't feel disdain for those who still miss who He is. We Christians tend to berate them, tend to characterize them as enemies of our faith. Actually, they're candidates to receive the gift of faith — and we should be praying like crazy. We should be bombarding heaven in our prayers because we've received the gift of faith. "God, give people the gift of faith today. Please God, give them the gift of faith you gave me."

God is not against them. He's an incarnate God. He understands them. He knows what they're going through. He knows why they're confused. He knows there's an enemy trying to blind them from seeing the truth, trying to darken their minds and hearts, setting up barrier after barrier. Let's not set up any more barriers. Let's remove the barriers, by way of love and kindness, by being others-centric. It's not all about me; it's not all about my rights: "They're coming against the rights of the Church." No. They're blind. They haven't had the revelation of faith. Our hearts should break over this, not make more demands. I don't need more for me. I need more for them.

Dear God, open the eyes of those who are blind, that they might see.

Faith is impossible. You can't make it happen. Faith is a gift from God. It is not a gift to God. It's not me giving a wonderful gift from my heart: "Here, God, let me give you my gift of faith." On the contrary, God has something to give me. It's called faith. Once I receive it, I don't claim it as something I came up with. I can only say, "Thank you for giving me this gift."

Mary looked right at Jesus and still didn't see Him — until that gift of faith was planted in her heart. There's nothing we can do to merit salvation. I may want to believe, but I have to pray, "Help my unbelief."

I've been a Christ-follower a long time, but there are moments when I'm still trying to figure this out. When I see difficult situations in my world, I find myself asking, "What in the world are you doing, God? I don't understand. I'm lacking faith. I want to believe, God; help my unbelief. Give me the gift of faith. Pour it on. I need more faith because I'm losing it. *I need you to fill me back up with faith so I can see as you do.*"

Mary Magdalene is standing in the midst of the greatest sign of God's love, power, and wisdom in human history — and she's reading it as a disaster. He made promises, she forgot. We are good at forgetting His promises. We're good at not seeing what He's doing. It looks like a disaster to us. But it's going to look way different when it's all said and done. It looked like the worst moment ever when Jesus died on the cross. It looked like the end of hope for the human race. For those folks hoping for a Messiah to set up a kingdom on earth, this was devastating. But Jesus says, "Wait and watch what I'm going to do. I'm going to rise from this tomb. I'm going to ascend back to my Father. I will prepare a place for you. I will make it possible for you to be a son or a daughter of my Father. I'm His Son; you can be too. I'm going to make this terrible thing beautiful. Let me give you a gift of faith. Let me help you see it differently."

We're too deep into the chaos of our world today to see it clearly. We're constantly complaining. I'm doing my share of it. We're feeling so much angst, with all the disruptions in the world, that we're missing what God is doing. He's in the midst of it. He's in the middle of the disaster, and He's going to turn it into beauty. He's going to turn it into victory — if the people of faith can ask Him for more faith.

We can find racial reconciliation in this moment like never before in the history of America. We stand on the precipice of a breakthrough, a miracle. Disaster? No. God is in the middle of it saying, "No, it's beauty. It's miraculous. It's resurrection. Let me show you how to embrace this. Let me show you how to love people through it. Let me show you how to incarnate yourself into it. I'll help you if you'll let me."

We look at our circumstances and conclude, "God's not there." But it's not because it's true; it's because *we can't see Him.*

We're Mary Magdalene.

We are people of faith in the middle of a world that's going crazy. How do we find our way? *Where are you, God?* He's right here. He's incarnate. I need to pray more. I need to say, "Show me, God. Give me faith to see you."

Mary missed Him. But then Jesus broke through.

Mary heard Him. When He called her "Woman," it didn't sound like Him. When He called her by her name, it sounded like Him: loving, kind, gracious. Jesus calls us by name. He speaks to us gently. He's not mean-spirited, reminding us of our failures. He's already covered our sins. He's reaching out to us. When Mary heard that voice — His loving voice, His personal connection — she recognized Him right away.

Jesus chose Mary Magdalene to be the first to understand that He was risen from the dead. A woman, not a man — in a male-dominated world. A scandal-ridden person — but He saw her as special. Precious. A reformed prostitute becomes the first messenger of the New Testament church. Not a pillar of the community, not an officer of the state.

Jesus has a divine priority of grace. He is showing us what the Father is like. "Let me show you. You got problems? I'm here to help you. You've had a broken life? I'm here to heal you. I'm here to give you power. I'm here to make everything right."

The Father is reaching out to broken people. Not to review their past. Not to count up the demons they've dealt with. Not to measure how much addiction they've succumbed to. Not to scold them for their doubt and unbelief. Not to grouse about how many times they missed Him, how often they didn't see Him when He was right there.

The Gospel is not that the good are in and the bad are out. It is that the humble are in and the proud are out. When we humble ourselves and acknowledge our need, He receives us. When we harden ourselves, when we live as if we know it all, we're right and others are wrong, then we're hindered by our own hardness. Not his. Ours. The Father is saying, "Come on, I'm here for you. Look at me, see me. I will give you the gift of faith to receive it."

The humble are in. Jesus starts with children. *Let the children come to me.* The grownups don't get it. "We got stuff to do, Jesus. Don't mess with these kids." Jesus cops a different attitude: "No, this is what it's about." Jesus starts with children. With prostitutes. With tax collectors. With thieves. With blind beggars. With the homeless. With the mentally ill. With the despised ethnic minority.

Then He's executed as a criminal. This is the path to salvation? But God wants us to know it's a broken world everywhere we go, and He is here to help, to fix, to heal. "All you have to do is accept me, humble yourself — and then let that love shine through the way you treat other people."

We're driven by a vision of power, of conquest. We want to be the know-it-alls whose superior wisdom causes everyone else to bow in awe before our point of view. Jesus took a different approach: "Let me serve you."

He was asked, "How do you get great in this kingdom of yours?" His answer: "Become the servant of all." What? No political office. No bully pulpit. No dictating the rules?

Something different: Serve the people around you, no matter what, no matter who they are, where they are — and you'll be great. *You'll look like me.*

When I recognize my brokenness, when I see that I am not better than the person I've been looking down on, then I'm ready to do God's work. *We need to kill our snobbery.* The ones who are serving are the ones revealing their faith. The ones who don't think they need forgiveness, the ones who make demands about what everybody else should do, will spin their wheels in frustration. The ones who humble themselves and recognize their brokenness can change the world, can love this world into wholeness, because that's what Jesus does.

In the garden, standing outside the tomb, Mary tries to hold Jesus. He stops her. He can't stay. He has more work to do. There's eternity ahead. He's looking ahead to His ascension. He's eager to tell the Father, "That's one of my brothers, that's one of my sisters."

28

DAZED

It is disorienting, even shocking, the first time you realize you're not the center of the universe. The first time you realize that every person you pass in the park is your brother or your sister.

Coming off the streets, I was only semi-coherent. It wasn't because I had fallen ill or suffered abuse or gone hungry. It was simply because I could not really find the words to communicate what I had experienced. Not what I had experienced physically, but what I had experienced spiritually.

I look back now at the transcript of my remarks in church, that first weekend back, and I see how dazed I was.

Maybe the truest, clearest thing I said were these 19 words:

"It's been an amazing journey. It really is going to take a while to unpack what I have experienced."

(I'm still unpacking.)

My pacemaker told me how amazing it really was. I had my heart fitted with a pacemaker some years ago — a remarkably run-of-the-mill surgical procedure in this age of high-tech medicine. One of the features of this life-sustaining gizmo is that it signals you when it needs attention: it needs a new battery, or it's not functioning properly. As I spoke to our church that weekend, my pacemaker "went off." I knew from the nature of the signal that it wasn't a life-threatening problem. But I had to wonder what this meant on a spiritual plane. Maybe I'd been under more stress, out on the streets, than I realized? Or maybe my heart had simply broken — finally — for broken people?

I told our church family: "The lessons — some I feel I've learned, and some I feel I have yet to learn, to figure out all of the things that I've seen and heard and experienced. I hope you bear with me. This is just the beginning of where we'll go together, what I feel like God will help us to learn together and grow in the experience."

Those words were truer than I knew.

The day would come when I had to return to the streets, to become homeless yet again.

29

GOING BACK

"Been there, done that."

You don't want to do it again.

I never imagined, when I first headed out to the streets, that I would ever "become homeless" again.

But what I imagined, and what actually happened, were two different things. Even after just one week on the streets, I felt drawn to the people there, and I had to stay.

And after I returned to my comfortable home and ministry and life, the streets — the memory of them, and my feelings as I drove through the city — were markedly different than they had been before.

Something in me was still there.

A year later, I found myself thinking about going back.

Coming off the streets, there was a sensitivity in my heart, like a cut or a scrape, that took a long time to heal. But it did heal, gradually. I felt the difference. I felt the distance. I was my comfortable self, more and more. I was less and less "with" the broken people in spirit.

It's easy to revert to old patterns of feeling and thinking. You have to tend a garden, or it grows up in weeds.

My weeds were coming back.

I resisted the notion. It seemed like such a stunt. Showboating. I pushed the idea out of my mind. I had so much work to do. So much ministry to manage.

Another year went by. But I couldn't get away from the idea of going back.

This time, there was no $300,000 fundraising campaign. There was no project, no social media presence. I didn't tell people in advance. Cathy knew, and a few others, and that was it. I wanted to experience again what people on the streets are experiencing. I wanted to move back into that world of reality, where people are struggling to survive difficult situations. I kept warning myself not to make this something it wasn't, not to over-spiritualize it — but it sure felt like God calling.

I set aside a week on my ministry calendar — a luxury no homeless person enjoys. One week only, assuming I would acclimate more quickly this time, understanding the basics of survival. I knew stuff now! I could cruise alleys for sleeping sites!

Oh yes, I remember this. This is uncomfortable. This is inconvenient. This hurts. This is scary.

Each step of the way, my sense-memory of my earlier excursion came washing back, like raw sewage.

But the people — the beauty of the souls, the loveliness of the humanity — it was all more radiant than ever. I heard the echo of what God had spoken into my spirit before: *Every person is precious.*

There was no media coverage. I didn't tell my church family I was going. I didn't have anyone checking in on me by phone every day. I didn't take a tent, only a sleeping bag. It rained. It was miserable.

I went back to find my preferred place, behind the abandoned industrial building, protected by the fence, near the dumpster. But the fence had been torn down. The alley was wide open; there wasn't even the illusion of protection.

I kept getting kicked out of places. (In certain areas, you learn the security officers' schedule, and you get there after their routine, instead of before.) I thought I was hiding, but the cops know where to look. They were kind, but they did their duty. I had to move.

I was more tired than ever. And I realized that thousands of homeless people live this way not just for a week, but every single night, for months or years. I slept in three different locations over the course of seven nights.

I was anonymous. I was homeless. I was a shrug of someone's shoulders.

Maybe I was seeing the world as God sees it: a bunch of people who don't care enough about each other.

I hope I learned more, my "second time out," than I did the first time.

I found myself going back in my mind, more than once, to Proverbs 14:31: "Whoever oppresses a poor man insults his Maker, but he who is generous to the needy honors him."

Only now, I was "the poor." I was "the needy."

Many times, I remembered my former self, looking down on the poor. Back in those days, I never thought of myself as showing contempt for my Maker. Making fun of God? Not me. But now, I saw things differently. Looking down on the poor, even despising them, or just failing to treat them with kindness — it's easy to get there.

I was struck again by the number of people on the streets dealing with mental illness. They seem to be beyond help. But I also found myself wondering: Can I be compassionate toward someone I don't understand? Wouldn't a gentle, caring response to this person be like Jesus?

A toilet can be a gift. I needed one. I looked at the Hyatt, across from the state Capitol building, wishing I could go in there and use the restroom. Suddenly it occurred to me: *Anyone can walk in there and use the restroom.* But because I was homeless, I had begun to think of myself as undesirable. I wouldn't even walk in there.

Thank God for Starbucks! They have restrooms they let you use!

I was no hero. I realize this. I had people from my church lurking in the shadows, making sure I was safe. Homeless people don't have such a security force. I knew I could pull the plug at any moment and head home to Cathy. But even with all my advantages, I felt once again the enormous burden of homelessness, of brokenness, that multitudes are experiencing every evening as the sun sets.

Not to be indelicate, but here's the bottom-line truth: It sucks the life out of you.

30

QUAGMIRE

It made the national news, some years ago. But since then, this type of story has become common. A police officer involved in a shooting.

Stephon Clark was 20-something. A story now regarded as typical: broken car windows, kid running down the streets, cops give chase, jumping fences, someone's backyard, helicopters, searchlights, someone zips around a corner in the dark, someone yells "Gun! Gun!"

Someone shoots someone.

Turns out, it was just a cell phone in the guy's hand.

He was at his grandparents' house.

Stephon's brother became a vocal protester, but his own behaviors could be described as erratic.

It was a mess.

Sacramento was on red alert.

By this time, I had done quite a lot of work in the Black community. I've been passionate about bringing our community together across racial lines. Diversity is a hallmark of our church. The unrest in our metropolitan area was a heartache for me. One night, marches blocked off entrances to the freeway.

I decided to attend some meetings of the City Council in support of initiatives that might make things right.

The first day I participated, the meeting was overwhelmed by protesters representing the African American community.

I was the only white minister who showed up. It was a picture of how things sometimes roll in a community, the separation of interests.

I spoke to the issues in one of the meetings the best I could.

Then came the funeral: a huge media event, of course. I offered to host the funeral at our church, but the family opted for a church in their South Sacramento neighborhood. The tensions in the community were running high, and the church was overrun.

I attended.

The controversy in our community was painful. Everyone had an opinion.

He shouldn't have run.

He broke out some windows.

You kill a guy for broken windows?

Our city was trapped in the quagmire mixture of two ingredients: (1) law enforcement and (2) what happens to Black men.

The dialogue in our community was noisy. Raucous.

I was not willing to speak into the politics, but our church cares about people. I felt it was important to be present at the funeral.

Things got crazy.

The dead man's older brother, Stevante Clark, threw himself across the casket. Sharpton put his arm around the man and calmed him down.

Fast forward several months. Our church is reaching out to people in need in Cesar Chavez Park. We offer sneakers. There's Stevante, receiving a pair of shoes. I found myself in conversation with him. He ended up coming to services at our church.

Some of my friends at church were nervous. *Isn't this the guy who went crazy at the funeral?* But I stood firm. We would love this guy. And he didn't act erratic at all around us. We offered scholarships to our school for his brother's small children.

I felt satisfied that we were doing what we could, which is not cause for self-righteousness. This is only a way of sleeping peaceably at night. *We loved people.*

I have said from the pulpit of my church, time and time again, that we support *both* law enforcement *and* people tragically affected with loss of life in their families. This is not a matter of choosing one or the other. The question is, How can we support the entire community? Both parties feel the pain. It's real.

Our walk must be careful. Our work is delicate. If we were God, we wouldn't struggle to know the way. But we're not. So all we can do is turn to Him, plead for His guidance, and keep doing our best to love people the way Jesus does.

I've become convinced of this, however: In every situation, when politics intrudes, we must take the political and turn it into the pastoral.

After years of ministry in an ethnically and culturally diverse community, I find that I have some favor in the Black community. People generally know if you're genuine, if you authentically care, and I do. I'm not trying to get anything from my interactions with the African American community. I'm trying to serve. Trying to love and care for people. Trying to identify with what they're experiencing. Trying to incarnate, like Jesus did. Trying to appreciate the pain they're feeling. Trying to appreciate the history feeding the Black community's pain.

But after all I've seen and experienced, I can only promote the pastoral. Government may have answers, politics may be important; but my focus has to be on the pastoral. *How does Jesus see this situation?*

31

THE VALUE OF SADNESS

My saddest moment on the streets?

I don't know.

Maybe at Loaves & Fishes, when Sister Libby's house guide said — apparently without intending to make some particular impression — that the population they're serving had changed.

In the 1970s and '80s, "it was single men" on the streets.

"Now, it's whole families."

The shift in the economy, the shift in what and how the government provides for the poor, has "changed everything."

And since the pandemic, it's "even worse."

Sadness is everywhere. But if it can motivate us, it can be valuable.

I have toured the Holocaust museum in Jerusalem. It is sobering. They tell the story, beginning to end: Naziism's rise, the war, the extermination of six million Jews. Even seeing the history in this stark, direct way, I was still unable to grasp the inhumanity. What was the goal? It was an ethnic cleansing. The Jews had to be eliminated. There was a parallel, for me: Here in America, to slavery, and with African Americans. They did not have to be eliminated, however — if they could be subjugated.

A person has to want to understand it.

Many of us want to distance ourselves from this issue.

(A movie like *Selma* drags it all back up for me.)

Black people are trying to find a path of acceptance in our society, but the system — our law and our community norms — are putting them down: beating, imprisoning, killing African American people.

For what?

When people march peacefully, asking a simple question — *Can't we have a place in this society?* — my heart responds.

This has become my life.

32

POLITICAL, OR PASTORAL?

What does systemic mean?

It means dads gone missing. Not just in our generation. Slave owners took Black fathers from families, then abused the wives who remained.

Black families had to survive this treatment.

Today, I hear many whites suggesting that *Black men don't care about their families*. But a lot of this behavior was *sown into the fabric* of African American families. During slavery.

Today, there are "poverty pockets." Look at homes in Beverly Hills, as recently as the 1960s, when a deed of trust might still specify that the property could not be sold to a non-Caucasian. Only in 1968 were such racially biased covenants banned.

In many "protected" neighborhoods today, the language is still there, in the regulations. Some say the language is too expensive to pull out; the lawyers' fees would eat us alive. In others, the law as stated in the books is simply not enforced. But it's still there. It's the law.

And we wonder why Black people feel put down.

We wonder why neighborhoods are as they are.

This is what *systemic* is about.

One great question for me is: Why don't we feel secure enough in ourselves, in our faith, in our God, to acknowledge the problem?

I have many white friends who say: I didn't have anything to do with this problem, personally, so why should I apologize for it? It happened. Mistakes were made. Our culture has changed a lot.

Yes, I'm grateful for the progress we've made. But there's a lot of room for greater change. Is it more important for me to convince a person of color that their pain is unjustified — or is it more important for me to let that person know I understand this pain may be real, and, as a child of God, I care?

What can we do to change those systemic burdens, change neighborhoods, elevate people to where they can thrive?

I find myself drawn to events that represent our nation's long history of inappropriate treatment of non-whites.

I think of *Just Mercy*, the memoir of Bryan Stevenson, a lawyer, NYU prof, and activist who founded the Equal Justice Initiative. Among his many other huge achievements, he advocates for African American inmates. In Montgomery, Alabama, I visited an outdoor museum that Bryan created, with rustic monuments hanging from a structure in a park. On the structures are the names of people lynched, so that they may not be forgotten. I can't describe it, seeing this memorial, and how deeply moved and disturbed I was, that many people in "my" world today don't want to talk about this aspect of our history. To them, it doesn't matter, it doesn't exist. The fact that people in the Black community still carry this pain somehow *doesn't count.*

I have come to a new place: If I am willing to acknowledge someone else's pain, without judging the origins of their pain, it's very freeing. It's validating. They may not need me to do anything more than to say, *What can we do to come together now? What can we do in this moment?* But to ask this question is, in a way, a threat to the one who asks — because maybe there will be an answer.

Deep in my spirit, I feel the injustice. Injustice motivates me. I don't always know what I need to do about it, but something in me tells me that I need to do *something*, because that's who God is.

God is a God of justice.

Of course, as we understand His Word, He will carry out ultimate justice. But until then, we're not assigned to *injustice*. We're called to be about justice in our own world, to the extent that we can make justice happen. Loving mercy, acting justly, according to Micah 6:8: *He has told you, O man, what is good; and what does the Lord require of you but to do justice, and to love kindness, and to walk humbly with your God?*

I have lived my entire life in God's Word, but this, more than any other bit, has become my "life verse." I see, in the behavior of so many Christians, so little kindness. God, help me, help me to be kind to someone who has no one to be kind to them. But God, please *also* help me to be kind to someone who oppresses the poor. Kind to those who make fun of their Maker. Kind to those who disagree with me.

Some shudder when I talk about matters of public policy; I'm too "political" for them. But we need to be willing to be misunderstood in this way. Jesus was. On Palm Sunday, as He rode through Jerusalem, people thought He was making a political statement. He wasn't doing political work. He was doing pastoral work. He was speaking to a much bigger issue than just *who's gonna be King*. He was dealing with the sinful core of mankind. If we're going to be Jesus incarnate in our city, we'll have to ride the donkey into the same kind of misunderstanding. Sometimes, public policy issues overlap the realm of the pastoral. We'll have to be ready for society to say we're being political when in fact we're being pastoral.

Jesus got lonely. We may come to know a bit of that feeling. I may find I'm the only white guy in the room addressing the need to treat Blacks differently. I may be the only Evangelical in the room addressing issues of concern to the LGBTQ community. I may be the only person in the room advocating for the homeless. But my pastoral calling — not my job, as a member of the clergy, but my Micah 6:8 calling in Christ — requires that I go there. And keep going there.

33

GOD IN YOU

2020. Coronavirus, economic collapse, racial tensions, protests and violence, a vicious election campaign — it's been a brutal season for our nation, and our world.

There's a connection to our situation, in Acts 2, on the Day of Pentecost, where the Christians gathered, the Holy Spirit filled them, and they spoke in a variety of languages they had never learned. People from other regions heard their own languages being spoken, and they were astonished. Some cynically assumed they'd been drinking. Peter seized the moment and set them straight. This isn't a trick, and it isn't alcohol. This is the fulfillment of prophecy: God pouring out His Spirit in the last days, sons and daughters prophesying, young men seeing visions, old men dreaming dreams.

We could use an outpouring of the Holy Spirit, an outpouring of God's grace. We could do with seeing visions, dreaming dreams, seeing God's power change our world.

It has to start with us. But first we need to be filled. In our national season of conflict, of rage and heartache, of fear and pain, I've felt myself being emptied. I need to be filled. And what I need to be filled with is not the bilge of social media, not the angst of the nightly news, but the love and grace and power of the Holy Spirit.

When the Spirit fell on those believers, God was sending a phenomenal message: I'll be in you. I'll be with you. Each of you. Jesus has ascended to heaven, but now you'll be Jesus incarnate in your world. My Spirit will guide you. My Word and my work won't be the exclusive domain of religious leaders. You'll have the Word. You'll do the work. Each of you, as individuals.

And this is for everyone. Every language group. Every person, from every walk of life. The Holy Spirit didn't fill each person so they could spend the rest of their lives looking out for their own interests. They spoke the languages of others. When I'm filled with the Spirit, my life isn't all about me anymore. It's about others. I start looking for people in need just like Jesus did. I'm the one doing His work here now.

Filled with the Spirit, I ask *How can I help you? How can I heal you? What can I do to liberate you?* No blame. No judgment. Just a passion for people in need.

Jesus was King. He could have lorded Himself over people. Instead, He took on the role of a lowly servant. When I'm filled with His Spirit, I lose my sense of superiority. I don't consider my color the best color, my culture the best culture. I'm doing something Jesus did: something called *grace*.

34

MY BIAS

Pastor Samuel Gordon, an African American on our church staff for more than two decades, has really helped me. He's been gracious and patient with me, helping me understand the perspectives, the pressures, the priorities of the Black community. It was challenging, especially at first, when our church family wasn't as racially diverse as it is today. Samuel had served as principal in predominantly African American schools in the inner city; he came to lead our church's school, which was predominantly white. But he has served faithfully and well. Much of what I understand about race relations today I've learned from Pastor Samuel.

Racism exists — we know this. People may debate where and how and why, but it clearly exists. And it's simple. One color of people looks at another color of people and says *We're better than you.* And they take advantage of this superiority. Acknowledging the existence of racism is the first step toward eliminating it.

As a white person, I may insist that I'm not racist; but it will be good for me to ask myself, *Is there some implicit bias in me?* When I see a non-white person, is there some kind of trigger inside me that adjusts my interactions with them? I need to search my own heart, and keep searching my own heart.

No, I'm not responsible for what happened to people of color a hundred years ago, but I have to acknowledge that a whole lot of really bad things *did* happen at the hands of white people. The inhumane treatment of Blacks' forefathers is not debatable; it's factual, and we should look that reality square in the face. Racism rooted itself in our society, and if I'm unwilling to admit it, I'm contributing to it.

The *how* of eliminating racism is not simple. It's complicated. It's work. But as we form and maintain healthy relationships with people who don't share our skin color, conversation and even cooperation can happen. *What do you think?* is a potentially powerful question.

I stepped into a dark hallway, in our church office complex, with a couple other members of our staff. Pastor Samuel happened to be at the far end of the hallway. One of my companions called out to him: "Hey, smile so we can see you!" It seemed funny at the moment, and Pastor Samuel seemed to roll with it. But now, I look back at that moment, and I realize that the line was not cool. Much later I learned that Pastor Samuel quietly took my companion aside.

"Because we're in relationship, I understand where you were coming from, that you didn't mean that in the way I heard it," he advised his friend. "But to say that to another African American in that context, that would offend them."

The staff member was mortified. "Oh, man, I didn't know," he admitted. And he apologized.

It was a moment of learning, part of the growth process — shedding light on white people's implicit bias.

When I hear loud music in the neighborhood, do I automatically think, "Is that African American family playing that loud music?" If I see a Black man coming down the street wearing a hoodie, will I cross the street because he looks like trouble, like a threat, because of something I've seen on television? These are biases. When I say, "You are really pretty for an African American woman," that's a bias. She's not just pretty — her beauty is qualified by her race. Unconscious bias. And if a Black person gently, graciously calls me out for my bias, I need to own it.

Some say apologizing for systemic racism goes too far. I think the opposite is true: Apologizing doesn't go far enough. We can't simply apologize and hope the issue goes away. We need to listen, and take action, standing with our African American brothers and sisters rather than remaining still and silent. Christian churches should be taking the lead on this.

We've seen lots of controversy about the slogan "Black lives matter." Some insist that all lives matter. But this is a given. There's no pushback about all lives mattering.

Black lives haven't mattered as much as other lives — so it's important to say black lives matter. It won't be true until we make it true.

Pastor Samuel tells a story of his father. When he was just five or six years old, he and his brother were playing outdoors. White guys drove up in a truck, jumped out, and tried to snatch them — the classic start of a lynching. But a white woman saw them, ran into her house, picked up the family shotgun, and ran back outside, firing it in the air. The assailants released the boys and drove off in a hurry. Black lives matter — but this is a truth that must be insisted on, because of our long national history of hate.

Racism is not a new problem, but video is a new revealer of the problem. So awareness is at an all-time high. In this way, whites are just now beginning to experience, at least vicariously, the oppression that Blacks have suffered for generations.

Pastor Samuel has six grandsons. Each one will get the same lecture that Samuel got as a boy: "When a police officer approaches you, you look him in the eye and say, 'Yes, sir … no sir.' Keep your hands on the wheel. Keep your hands out of your pocket."

I didn't have to give my own sons such a lecture. We're white.

Samuel's son LaRon landed a college basketball scholarship. He was excited to go. In his first week, his wallet was stolen in the team locker room. He complained to the coach, but nothing was done. LaRon wouldn't let it go. "This is wrong," he said. "This shouldn't happen." He wrote a letter to the university president. "I'm not just experiencing this in the locker room," he said, "but on the campus. I'm getting dirty looks in the cafeteria. I hear them telling jokes. I've heard them use the N-word." He asked for a meeting. The president brought him in, and listened. The university made some changes. But LaRon's pain didn't just evaporate. It didn't seem right that you should have to push so hard just to be treated like a white person — not in America. For a long time, LaRon couldn't say the Pledge of Allegiance. It felt false. The flag is supposed to represent liberty, but there's a liberty gap for Black people. It's systemic: It's about unemployment, poverty, healthcare. Where can I live? Why is there no grocery store in this neighborhood? What kind of education will my child get in this school? Why are things so different for Black people? How is this fair? How is this right?

As a pastor, responsible for shepherding a flock of believers, I have to urge people out of their comfort zone, to listen and learn. I'm trying to listen to the voice of God. I'm trying to hear His heart in the voices of Christian leaders: T.D. Jakes, Judah Smith, A.R. Bernard, Dr. Tony Evans, and others.

Listening and learning are humbling. I have to be willing to die to myself, my pride, my self-assurance, my preconceived notions. I need a heart of humility. And I need the courage to face the possibility that I'm not entirely right. I need to be willing to admit that *I could be better*. Vulnerability isn't comfortable. And it isn't automatic. But it's critically important.

If the people of a church are willing to say, "Yes, there is racism here, and it's not right," they can change — and they can begin to impact their community. Changed communities can change whole regions. Our world can change. But it has to start with me, with us. Is this America's tipping point, where huge change begins?

I believe healing is possible. Healing can begin if we can all embrace each other, across racial lines, and declare that each of us matters equally to God — and to each other.

35

THE BADGE I WEAR

Embracing isn't the trend today.

Divisiveness is the trend.

Christians are right there in the scrum with everybody else, fighting for rights and proclaiming privileges. *You can't tell me what to do.*

We saw it in the pandemic, with the simple issue of mask-wearing. I didn't want to wear a mask; I never liked them. But at the same time, I understood that wearing a mask was an expression of concern for others. In this way, it was a good thing for me to do. Not everyone agreed! Some fumed that the government was assuming too much control over our personal lives. Some claimed that the entire pandemic was a hoax — or that the media had artificially magnified the crisis in order to influence elections — or simply that masks were powerless to arrest the spread of the virus. On the other hand, to a healthcare worker in ICU dealing with people who contracted the virus — to the families of hundreds of thousands killed by the virus — the pandemic could hardly be regarded as a hoax. And mask-wearing could hardly be regarded as an insufferable burden.

I found myself more and more deeply grieved by the bickering, and its relentless ferocity. Even as I stood before my congregation and tried to sort it out, it was extremely hard for me even to express what I was feeling.

How could we as a church family, as followers of Christ, find a way to come together rather than divide? How could we honor God and honor others without compromising the standards of Scripture? How could we do what was right? *What was right?*

Embracing each other can seem impossible.

Politics a century ago was "the art of the deal": compromise, "horse-trading." Today, politics is predicated on the idea of conquest. Crush your opponent. This concept moves us farther and farther from each other. And the deepening political divide is tragically affecting the Church. We have allowed politics to infect our faith.

We have Democrats, Republicans, and independents in our church. *But my political party is not the badge I wear when we gather in the house of God.* Many of my Evangelical brothers and sisters will disagree with me about this. They have come to believe that a good Christian must support a certain view of government. But this isn't how Jesus operated.

No matter what political party you belong to, you belong to a monarchy — with a King who loves you, and who always acts in your best interests. My King has placed me in a Kingdom that will never end, a Kingdom that is not of this world. My King is Jesus, and He gives me the grace to live in perfect peace as I keep my mind and heart fixed on Him — no matter what leaders the citizens of my country have chosen. *It is legitimate for you and me, as fellow Christ-followers, to disagree about which government policy is wiser or more effective or even more reflective of the heart of God.* What's *not* legitimate is for you and me, as fellow Christ-followers, to demonize each other, to savage each other, because of our views on government policy. (It's a privilege of democracy that you and I both have opportunities to influence public policy; Jesus didn't live in a place of such freedom.)

I don't consider myself to be liberal *or* conservative. I consider myself to be accountable. Jesus was labeled "too liberal" when He defied the laws of the Pharisees. Then he was labeled "too conservative" for teaching standards that some folks didn't want to comply with. In truth, He wasn't liberal or conservative. He was God's Son.

We need to be known as followers of Jesus. Not primarily identified with one ideology or another.

When Jesus stands in the temple in Luke 4:18, reading Isaiah 61 from the scroll, He switches the prophetic words into the present tense: "The Spirit of the Lord is upon me, because he has anointed me to proclaim good news to the poor. He has sent me to proclaim liberty to the captives and recovering of sight to the blind, to set at liberty those who are oppressed."

This is the mission of Jesus. The mission hasn't changed. It's ours now, too. This is what you and I are anointed to do: proclaim good news — *really* good news — to the poor. In our culture today, we see *bad* news being proclaimed to the poor. Negativity aimed at the poor. Judgment heaped upon the poor.

Jesus takes a different approach. "I've come to give good news to the poor," He says. "There's a way out. You don't have to stay stuck in a place of poverty."

Christ's mission — our mission — is to lift up anyone who is poor. To set at liberty those who are oppressed. Yes, *there are oppressed people in our culture today.* Our culture is not color-blind. If we are clear-minded, open to the truth, we can look at our nation's history and understand that some of our people have been oppressed by our systems of government — over the course of some 400 years.

Jesus goes on to read about proclaiming "the year of the Lord's favor" — the "jubilee year." Say to the oppressed, "You're free." Say to the slave, "You're no longer enslaved." Say to those who have been in a deeply dark place, because of how society has treated them, "I will help you step into the light."

This is not just a "Black problem." This is a Latino problem, an Asian problem, a Native American problem — a problem that white people have not adequately grappled with over the centuries.

And it's a problem that the Church has not adequately taken a lead on it.

In Amos 5:23-24, God's people have been celebrating, worshiping, making their showy ceremonial sacrifices, rejoicing in their special relationship with the Father.

But the Father isn't having it.

"Take away from me the noise of your songs," He says; "to the melody of your harps I will not listen."

Their attitude isn't right. Their spirit is wrong. So their "worship" doesn't count. What's the alternative? What's the Father's priority? What does He really want from these exuberant worshipers?

"But let justice roll down like waters," He commands, "and righteousness like an ever-flowing stream."

Sure, they bring their sacrifices, but they're harming others along the way. They're leaving the oppressed in their dark places. They don't care about the poor, the broken, the lost. They're living in an us-and-them world, they don't care about "them."

Could it be that God doesn't care about our "joyful noise" if we're not practicing compassion and justice?

We solemnly quote our Pledge of Allegiance: "and justice for all." But we don't live it. This hasn't been a land of justice for all. It's been a land of justice for me.

36

CAN'T AFFORD IT

Dr. Nicole Martin earned a Doctor of Ministry degree at the highly respected Gordon-Conwell Theological Seminary. Not long after Michael Brown was killed in Ferguson, Missouri, she was invited to participate in an event with several leading pastors. Waiting in the "green room" before going onstage, she found herself — a Black woman — sitting next to the white pastor of a prominent megachurch. In such a context, in the flow of conversation, it was natural for her to ask him: "What are you saying about race from your pulpit?" He politely responded, "Let's not get into that right now."

"That just didn't satisfy how I felt," Dr. Martin recalls.

I'll paraphrase their conversation.

"I'm sorry," she said to the pastor. "I know we don't have a lot of time, but I'd like to know what keeps you from telling people in your congregation to care about me?"

"Well, if I can be honest," he replied, "I can't *afford* to say something."

"What does that mean, afford?" she inquired.

"I've got board members that have already sent me letters," the pastor answered, "stating 'If you say something about this on Sunday, you'll be removed from your pulpit.' I have big donor families that have said, 'If you speak up on this, we'll take our money and go elsewhere.' I acknowledge this is horrible and sinful and wrong, but I've got kids and a family. This church is all I have."

Fear is a huge motivator. As a Christ-follower, called to His mission of compassion and justice, I have to ask myself: *What are you afraid of?*

When the Governor of California issued an order banning church services during the pandemic, some members of our congregation were upset that I didn't lead the church in defiance of the order, because the Governor was taking away our religious liberties. But this decree — which was about health, not faith — and it was temporary, not the end of the world — did not hinder my ability to express my love for God. My religious liberties were not at risk. But fear of losing religious liberties drove many to anger, and lawlessness.

Fear and anger also energized plenty of pandemic-era fundraising.

Yes, I felt fear too. I know people vote with their feet, and their checkbook. People could quit the church. We could lose ground financially and find ourselves hindered in doing the work of God. But ultimately, I had to take the risk of standing firm.

What am I afraid of? Will fear turn me into a "noisy songs" Christian who misses the Father's priority of compassion and justice? Do I have the courage to care about a person who's hurting or frightened because of how people of their racial group are being perceived in the media? Am I willing to say "I care about you"?

In this age of social media, many of us have become more skilled dart-throwers. We need to put down the darts. Let our divisive words fall silent. Stop fighting. See that people are hurting, and — rather than analyzing whether their pain is justified — simply lament their pain. Sympathize. Care. Love.

After my backyard accident, recovering from a fractured skull and collarbone, all the various members of my family came to visit me. They were healthy, they had every reason to celebrate life, but they couldn't. Why not? Because someone they loved was hurting. Someone they cared about was in a dark place. All they could do was surround me and pray for me, and lament my situation.

There are people all around us in the same lamentable condition: broken, hurting, in need of healing. We Christians prefer to celebrate, worship, make a joyful noise — but we need to pause and feel some sorrow. We need to lament the pain of those who are in pain.

37

A LAMENT

Lament acknowledges suffering. In the Bible, lament is a liturgical response to the reality of suffering. Lament engages God in the context of trouble and pain. And lament contains an element of hope. The hope of lament is that God will respond to the suffering that is being acknowledged through the sorrow of our heart.

Lament isn't popular. But lament is healthy. It's helpful. It's needed.

After the brutal death of George Floyd, the level of awareness of our racial history was suddenly dramatically elevated. Anyone who saw video of the killing had to be affected by it. Moreover, millions understood, many for the first time, the need for sorrow. There was an automatic, widespread response of lament.

But then came the efforts to dismiss it. *George Floyd had a criminal history. George Floyd had drugs in his system.* We instinctively resist lament — so powerfully that we will make excuses for ghastly brutality. Every human being has a history of blemishes. Or we cross the road, turn away, to avoid the issue altogether. *Come on, get over it.*

Who deserves to die the way George Floyd died? No one. Our excuse-making and evasion are born out of the injustice in our hearts — when in fact our hearts should break for the injustice of this tragedy.

For someone who has been oppressed, *get over it* isn't feasible. Because at the end of the day, they're still oppressed. They're still under the burden.

My lament has led me to new discoveries. I didn't know about Juneteenth — the June 19th observance of that day in 1865 when slaves in Texas finally got word that they were free. Lincoln had freed them legally nearly two and a half years earlier, but now, finally, it was real. Cause for celebration. In the Black community, the significance of Juneteenth is profound.

I didn't know about the 1921 "race massacre" in Tulsa, in America's wealthiest Black neighborhood, the "Black Wall Street." More than 35 square blocks of thriving Black-owned businesses were burned, and 26 Blacks killed. Didn't make it into my school history books.

I didn't know the sordid history of Mount Rushmore. The land still belongs to the Lakota (affirmed as recently as 1980 in a Supreme Court ruling) but was illegally taken from them when gold was found in the hills. The Native population was pushed out. The Mount Rushmore sculptor was deeply connected to the Ku Klux Klan. I remember being amazed, as a child, by this massive monument. I love my country. But discovering the Rushmore backstory hits me hard. What must the Lakota feel, when they look up at our Presidents' stone faces on the mountain?

I lament.

I was not familiar with the story of Ruby Bridges, the first Black child to integrate a public school in New Orleans, in 1960. She was six years old, going into the first grade. (I was three at the time. Her life and mine overlap.) The authorities wouldn't let Ruby into the school until November 14th. When they finally admitted her, all the white families kept their children home. No local teacher would teach her; a white teacher from Boston had to be brought in. As Ruby went back and forth between home and school each day, white families shouted profanities at her. (Ruby Bridges is a precious woman today, still advocating for change.)

It's not possible to learn what happened to little Ruby and say it doesn't mean anything today. What happened to Ruby was set in motion centuries before — and what happened to Ruby still happens, on innumerable levels, today. Which absolutely matters.

Lament is not simple. Lament acknowledges the complexities of life. Lament says, "Part of the pain I feel is because it's so hard to bring about change."

RICK COLE

I didn't know that 12 of our U.S. Presidents were slaveowners. Some of them had hundreds of slaves. Some of them treated their slaves with brutality.

Lament corrects the overemphasis on triumphalism. In our North American culture, we love success. We want to be healthy, wealthy, and wise. We love celebrity. We want the trumpet sounding. We focus on the triumphs. There's little room for lament.

How many Sundays could I preach a message like this? Not many. It feels heavy. It feels heavy to me while I'm writing it. I feel sorrow. I pray that after writing it, the burden will lift. I'm hopeful of this. Lament can lead us to praise. But in the meantime, we as the Church need to integrate a theology of suffering with our theology of celebration. *We can't rejoice only.*

Philippians 2:3 makes it so clear: "In humility count others more significant than yourselves." This is a life verse for me. If someone else is more significant than me, and that someone is hurting — broken — oppressed — it's right for me to lament. It's right for me to pursue justice for that person.

Will I?

38

THE PEOPLE I DON'T LOVE

Will I be homeless again? A third excursion in the streets? Sometimes I think I will. This doesn't feel *finished*.

I want to be sensitive to the Spirit's leading, and be willing to go. Broken people still matter to me — in fact, more than ever. Returning to them, to walk and listen and live among them for a time, seems right. I never want to lose my heart for them.

We'll see.

In the meantime, I'm still learning to love.

Among my spiritual struggles is self-righteousness — especially toward people I regard as self-righteous! I'm still learning to love the people I don't love.

Hardest of all: *church people*. The people I'm called to shepherd. When they don't function the way I think they should, I feel angry.

At which point, I'm trying to master the art of having a conversation without flipping out, or inciting *them* to flip out.

I have the capacity to shut people out very, very quickly.

How can I keep conversation going, keep it productive, dealing with people I don't agree with — or even like?

I can usually see someone else's issues more easily than I see my own. A few presidential election cycles ago, a member of our church staff turned up to work sporting a Bush sticker. "How many people are you trying to offend today?" I joked. He was puzzled. "Half the people you encounter today will look at your sticker and not want to talk to you. Our mission is to *reach* those people." It's not that our staff members shouldn't have political opinions, or support certain political personalities or movements; but that's not what we're focused on in the day-to-day work of our church.

We've become a country divided in the worst way by political parties, and much of the Church at large has actually bought into that division. I want to stay away from that. Our message is about Jesus — an eternal Kingdom, not a temporal one. If I can avoid pushing people's buttons — setting off a political debate — good. Many Christians today have adopted an in-or-out mentality: *If you don't believe like me politically, you're not a Christian.* I think Jesus is bigger than that. I'm trying to help people lay down the labels, and see souls, made in God's image. Everyone is precious to Him. When someone doesn't believe as I do, *they're still precious to Him.*

But I struggle. My nature is to judge that Christian, that church person, who has that in-or-out mentality. They're judgmental about others, so I'm judgmental about them! I'm trying to figure out how to put the *precious* label on them too.

How can I keep conversation going, not push them away, not cut them off, not drive a wedge — yet maintain my doctrine?

It's a daily challenge for me.

39

GAYS ARE PEOPLE TOO?

S ome hot buttons are hotter than others.

I've taken heat for my openness to the LGBTQ world.

Our church's message historically had been *They're going to hell.* But I found myself asking, *Doesn't God care about them?* Scripture says God wants none to perish, calls all to repentance. How can I communicate His love to a gay person if all they sense from my church is *You're not welcome here and you never will be?*

Prop 8 was coming up in California — it would legally define marriage as the union of a man and woman, barring gay marriage, in the days before the Supreme Court ruling allowing it. I was invited to write a viewpoint piece for the newspaper. I tried to communicate the scriptural position without being offensive; I hoped to express support for the measure but do so graciously.

The piece ran on the front page.

Our church already had some history with the gay community. Years ago, when my father was still pastor, a gay activist group had staged a protest at the church. Now, with my front-page article, we were front and center again.

But God has a way of making good out of our messes.

A nutritionist attending our church invited me to her workplace; her group serves the homeless population and AIDS patients. She wanted me simply to pray with the dying. I agreed. While I was there, she gave me a tour, introducing me to doctors and other staff, and the organization's leaders. Many looked at me sideways; wasn't I the "anti-gay" guy?

They happened to be forming a committee to pursue an audacious goal: Five Years to End AIDS. There were healthcare people, civic leaders, and others — but no clergy. They invited me to join. The board of directors would approve each committee member. When my name appeared, one fellow objected: *If he's in, I'm out.*

Those who had invited me prevailed on him to at least meet me. So we got together. Bart became my friend.

He's a gay guy, an activist, an administrator at a local hospital, about my own age. When I arrived for our meeting at a coffee shop downtown, the newspaper with my page 1 opinion piece, festooned with yellow highlights, was lying on the table. I began to assure him I had wanted to write something hopeful and inoffensive, but I obviously failed; offending was never my intention. But Bart waved me off. He just wanted to get to know me.

We found we had a lot in common. He had studied for the priesthood. He knows the Bible. In that hour together, we formed somewhat of a bond. Maybe we could talk some more, he suggested. I could help you understand the gay community better, and you could help me understand your world better.

We started meeting consistently. Bart unraveled some of the myths of the gay community, in the view of conservative religious people. We got into the issue of "born that way." As a healthcare professional, Bart was clinical and scientific. As a gay person, he could also address the subject anecdotally.

"When did you decide you'd be heterosexual?" he asked. Of course I didn't decide. "Same here," he replied. "I didn't decide I would be gay. It's all I remember."

As he shared clinical studies, I found my heart softening toward people I had often dismissed.

Our friendship developed. I cared about the guy. I was drawn to him as a soul.

He hadn't been inside a church in many years. But he happened to drive past our church every day on his way to and from work.

"We could meet at your office," he said one day. So we did.

We were having tremendous spiritual conversations, mostly on subjects he initiated.

One day, I laid a challenge before him: If you believe the Bible — which is where I'm at, and it's my job — there are Scriptures that talk about sexuality. I find myself in a hard spot. Our friendship is important to me. I care about you. I enjoy our communication. Our friendship is growing. But what the Bible says is still something I'm accountable to. I don't want a barrier between us. I'm struggling with how to stay true to what God says, and how to communicate with you so it doesn't undermine our relationship.

Bart might have gotten up and walked away forever. But he didn't.

"I never thought about that," he replied. He seemed to appreciate my dilemma.

"I know God cares about you," I said, "and I know I do too."

So we went to work on the problem — with hours and hours of conversation. For years, we met once a month.

Then my dad died, suddenly, a Valentine's Day heart attack. It was big news in the community, covered on television and in the press. A reporter called me for an interview, which lasted all of 20 minutes. Most of the resulting article was positive, but the "anti-gay" theme was featured. I called the writer to complain. *Gotta do my job* was the reply.

Bart saw the article and phoned me. Sometimes in the gay community, he said, "this kind of thing stirs people up." There could be a scene at the funeral. "I would hate for that to happen," he said. But if I didn't mind, he would be willing to "navigate" any negativity in the lobby. He would be the bridge, between "our" world and "theirs." I thanked Bart sincerely.

I saw Bart change over time. He didn't confess faith in Christ, the way we teach it. But I remain hopeful that he will embrace the love of God that leads to an eternal relationship with Him.

He transferred to Oakland, but we stayed in touch. Then came the Gay Pride Parade.

He invited me every year. "I'll talk you through it," he laughed. But the parade always happened on a Sunday, so I was able to beg off because of my pastoral duties. Finally one year, I agreed to take a Sunday off. Cathy and I headed to San Francisco and met Bart at the parade route.

At Glide Memorial Church — known for its acceptance of gays, with lots of outreach to the homeless and other needy groups — produced a full-blown worship service. It was dynamic! Then the parade itself started. Bart spent the day explaining things to us; he wanted me to see a different point of view.

(We met a street preacher who railed against homosexuality; Bart talked to him every year, on Parade day. I asked the man about his results: Anyone ever make a faith commitment? Not really, he replied. Maybe, I suggested, this isn't an effective method?)

Bart had come into my world, and invited me into his. I could go there, because I cared about him. I wanted him to know: I'm in this for you.

For a while afterward, I stood in my pulpit and communicated on Sundays that God's heart is for all people, that our church should be a place where gay people feel welcome, where they feel we love them; everybody belongs here. We need a different approach to communicating God's love, I said.

Some of our folks pushed back. Gays? You've gone too far.

40

WHAT LOVE LOOKS LIKE

I became homeless. I engaged with the gay community. We reached out to the African American community and ethnic minorities. We strove to choose the poor.

Our church has changed.

We're discovering what love looks like.

I think we over-complicate our faith. Jesus is good. If we can follow a path of goodness something like the way He followed a path of goodness, we can contribute well to our world.

I've heard people say they won't set foot in a church: *God would strike me with lightning!* They think of the church as a place where good people go. Bad people stay outside.

But we're all broken.

Today, our church family is more than racially diverse; it's diverse period. We have everyone from lifetime churchgoers to one-time murderers — with murderers leading prison ministries. We have the poor and the elite. And by God's grace, each seems to have growing empathy for the other.

I have a broken heart for broken people. If we can develop a broken heart for broken people — God's heart — we'll fulfill our calling in Christ.

A widowed grandmother launched a ministry for widowed women. You stop dreaming for yourself when you find yourself widowed, she says; but I started dreaming how to help hurting people. That beautiful, widowed grandmother happens to be my mom.

Some of our church members have started non-profit organizations to help the homeless. A member of our choir got together with some friends to launch a Burrito Walk — persuading Mexican restaurants to donate ingredients. They've taken on compassion where they wouldn't have before.

One of our pastors, who started as a small group leader, noticed an elderly Armenian tenant in his apartment complex who wasn't changing his burned-out lightbulbs. So he bought some lightbulbs and changed them himself. That act of kindness led to the birth of an Armenian-language church. The traditional Armenian faith tends to be heavily legalistic and harsh; but this ministry is full of grace. They also run a food pantry and help people with immigration.

Equal Start was an after-school program for inner-city kids. Many children in the neighborhood had never been outside of it. Our team took them to the University of Oregon, where they visited the Athletic Department and got a pep talk about going to college and practical advice on how to get there. Each kid got a "passport" to be stamped with each place they visited: Nike HQ, the beach, and more. The next year, Equal Start took the kids to USC. Pete Carroll was coaching there at the time; he met with them. And they went to Disneyland! One year they did it at Stanford.

In a local school, there was a teacher's lounge so ratty, the teachers wouldn't even go in. A team from our church renovated it, gave a Starbucks vibe. They ran a marathon to raise money for it. (I trained for that marathon; it was a painful experience.)

Character Combine was a ministry that taught life principles to coaches. Almost every high school in the city participated. The first year, 50 team coaches and captains participated. It got bigger every year, until there were 300 coaches and 500 students.

Evening of Dreams also produced a prom, pairing star athletes with children who have special needs; 250 "couples" enjoyed a spectacular evening.

We're bringing more inner-city kids to our Christian school, offering financial aid so it's not out of reach for their families.

The Alliance for Character and Educational Development (ACED) serves 40 children per year — kids at risk, living below the poverty line. Many have experienced real trauma. One saw his father killed. ACED kids have gone on to universities, some ended up at Harvard. One, from Honduras, attended a baseball clinic produced by one of our church members; the child's mother pleaded for someone to take him in, to keep him safe in America. One of our families took the boy in. He went to college, graduated, got drafted into Major League Baseball; today he's starting for the San Francisco Giants — the first-ever Honduran-born player in the MLB.

Our outreach team partnered with Fleet Feet, offering tennis shoes to homeless people. I was there — homeless — when they arrived in Cesar Chavez Park. Fifty pairs of shoes, organized by gender and size, were gone in five minutes. They also served sandwiches! It was a joyful day in the park.

We are finding ways to choose the poor. Finding ways to love the unlovely. Finding ways to restore broken people.

It's the work of being Jesus incarnate in our world, and it doesn't end. It just keeps getting better.

41

FIGURING OUT THE GOD THING

Being Jesus incarnate in my world is not only about connecting to people who are radically different from me.

It's also about my marriage. It's about how I treat my own children. It's how I have a conversation with a non-Christian stranger. It's about how I treat people in my own church, to their face and behind their back.

Relationally, our world is pretty messed up. Even the local church has its own brand of dysfunction. But if we don't allow ourselves to be stuck in our own current view, if we commit to lifelong learning, if we resist the notion that we already know everything we need to know, and that we're already doing everything we need to do, God will keep giving us new opportunities to be Jesus incarnate in our world.

And the world can change.

As I write these words, I'm 63 years old. But I am still trying to figure out the whole God thing, and how He can work in me, and how it relates to my world. How can I take my own faith experience and make it desirable to someone who has no interest in it, or even someone who's "anti-faith"?

I feel drawn to people who are angry at Christians and don't like the church. Let me talk to them. Is there any way I can help them see God differently? Not by shouting at them. Not by snarling on social media. Not by coercion. Not by legislation. How about by love?

I want you to see Jesus in a pure, unfiltered way. You, my co-worker. You, my friend. You, my neighbor. You, whoever you are — whoever God has brought across my path today.

How can I reveal Jesus to unsuspecting people?

How can I get myself into someone's else's shoes, and let my empathy do God's thing?

42

DID YOU FEED ME?

As I'm writing these words, a news headline scrolls across my computer: "Televangelist seeks millions to buy private jet."

I sigh.

As a church, we are called to be a compelling force for good. For broken people, we must serve with no apparent motive. We do it because it's right. Not for the jet.

If we can identify with marginalized, hurting people, they may come to reevaluate their notion of what it means to be a Christian.

"You always have the poor with you" (Matthew 26:11) is often quoted by those who do nothing to love, embrace, or help the poor. "You always have the poor with you" can become a crutch to hold up the lack of compassion.

Proverbs 13:41 calls on us to honor God by loving the poor. It also makes clear: If we don't love the poor, we're not honoring God.

Orthodoxy will not be the test of our godliness. The question in eternity will be "Did you feed me?"

The thoughts of Jesus — His actions when He served here on earth — have never made more sense to me.

My prayer is that we will somehow find a pathway to compassion for broken humanity — not to sit in judgment of them. It's not a path we can be pushed onto. But if my own story can open someone's heart a bit, to see the world a little differently, to inspire some connection to broken people, then my story will have been worthwhile.

Let's be incarnate. A moment of compassion — a lifetime of change.

THE END.

ACKNOWLEDGEMENTS

It all begins with the blessing of God's love poured out through Jesus' sacrifice to cover my brokenness. The experiences that led to this book have all been orchestrated through the wonder of being led by the Holy Spirit.

My family supported me every step of the way. Cathy has confirmed the mission of my efforts and released me to pursue these dreams. Nate, Laine, and Travis gave me strength by joining me at various times on the streets of our city and their passion for others inspires me.

My small group where the title for this book originated. Glenn Murray, Jud Riggs, Rick Pickering, Phil Oates and Larry Allbaugh have provided accountability and wisdom as I have processed the principles of my story. While sharing with them my experience of living on the streets, Glenn said one word, "Incarnate." From that word, the story unfolds.

Teresa Best, my personal assistant, has enabled me to stay on track with my day-to-day responsibilities. Her attention to detail is remarkable, matched only by her excellence of spirit to graciously interact with anyone who contacts my office. She has also provided editing expertise and has read through the manuscript several times with great attention to detail.

The team I work with at Capital Christian Center have shouldered the passion for our city along with me. Each of our Pastoral Staff members carry significant responsibilities in caring for our church members and they encourage me with their willingness to sacrifice for the mission.

Mike Messner prompted me to write my experiences in book form. He patiently waited until I was ready and then directed me to the right resources to help me bring this book to life. I would not be where I am today without Mike's wisdom and guidance along the way.

I am deeply grateful for Doug Brendel and his skill to coach me in moving what was inside of me to the printed page. His heart seemed to beat with mine as he helped me put words to what was in my heart.

Jason Batt has partnered with me for 18 years. With his heart for others, coupled with a high level of intellect, he has organized the process of bringing this project to publication. It takes a village, but Jason is a chief among the villagers.

Former Mayor of Sacramento, Kevin Johnson, opened the door for this story to come to life. His heart for the broken of our city moved me and his invitation to engage in reaching out in new ways changed me. His leadership and influence has made our city a better place to live and has made me a better person in caring for others.

Samuel Gordon has walked with me for the past 26 years. He has enabled me to understand the journey of my brothers and sisters who are a different color than me. I am still learning and it seems he is willing to walk with me for as long as it takes.

A number of men in our Capital Christian family assisted me to ensure my safety on the streets at night. Their love and willingness to sleep on the pavement provided me with a sense of security. Tom Platina made sure there was someone with me at night and provided needed wisdom for me to navigate the homeless experience.

Finally, I am moved by the love our entire Capital Christian Center family. I have been covered by the prayers of so many and encouraged by the willingness to grow with me. The path of life is filled with many joys and sorrows. Being able to share the journey with people who are committed to God and to one another makes miracles possible. Thank you, Capital family, for joining me in journey.

FOLLOW RICK COLE TODAY

facebook.com/revrickcole

twitter.com/revrickcole

instagram.com/revrjcole

www.CapitalOnline.cc

ABOUT RICK COLE

Do what is right, not what is easy. If anybody has taken this message to heart, it's Rick Cole. Over his 25 years as Senior Pastor at Capital Christian Center in Sacramento, Rev. Rick Cole has been an active ally for social justice, taking a hands-on approach to issues of racial reconciliation and homelessness in his community as well as serving countries all around the world by leading teams through global mission work. Cole pastors a congregation of over 3,000 members and leads a staff of 14 pastors in addition to 180 church and school employees. He is the co-author of two other books, *Souldesign: A Roadmap for Personal Growth* and *Souldesign: Living A Life of Love*. Rev. Rick Cole lives in California with his wife Cathy. They have three children and five beautiful grandchildren.

VISIT INCARNATEBOOK.COM

For more resources on:

Homelessness,

Racial Justice,

Beginning a Relationship with Christ,

and more ...

Capital

CAPITALONLINE.CC

CPSIA information can be obtained
at www.ICGtesting.com
Printed in the USA
LVHW010423280421
685771LV00003B/8/J

9 780985 085216